Oldchurch

the

Workhouse

Story

How it all began

Ian S. Moore

Published by Workhorse Productions
41, High Street,
Stock, Ingatestone,
Essex. CM4 9BN.

ISBN 0 9536155 0 2

Printed & Bound by Lavenham Press Ltd.,
Water Street,
Lavenham,
Sudbury,
Suffolk. CO 10 9RN.

CONTENTS.

Page

Preface. 7

New Brooms Sweep Clean. Essex, no Hills, but a Bottom of Clay. 9

The Guardians Elected. They Take the Helm. 17

Looking for Work. The Old Parish Workhouses and Selling Them Off. 25

Medical Officers and Medical Clubs. 33

One Workhouse or Two? Barking the Fishing Town; Ilford the Staging Post. 43

Buying the Land, Choosing the Builder. Romford and the Market; its Businesses and Shops. 55

Building the New Workhouse. 71

Hornchurch, Upminster, Cranham, Great Warley, Dagenham, Rainham, and Wennington and Havering, the Villages 81

Oldchurch Workhouse Opens. The Railway comes to Romford. Running the Workhouse, Pauper Offences, Milling Corn. 93

Emigration. The Pitcairn Scandal. The Failure of Johnsons Bank. 107

Workhouse to Infirmary; the Beginning. The Hungry Forties. 117

Postscript. 129

ROMFORD AND DISTRICT CIRCA 1850.

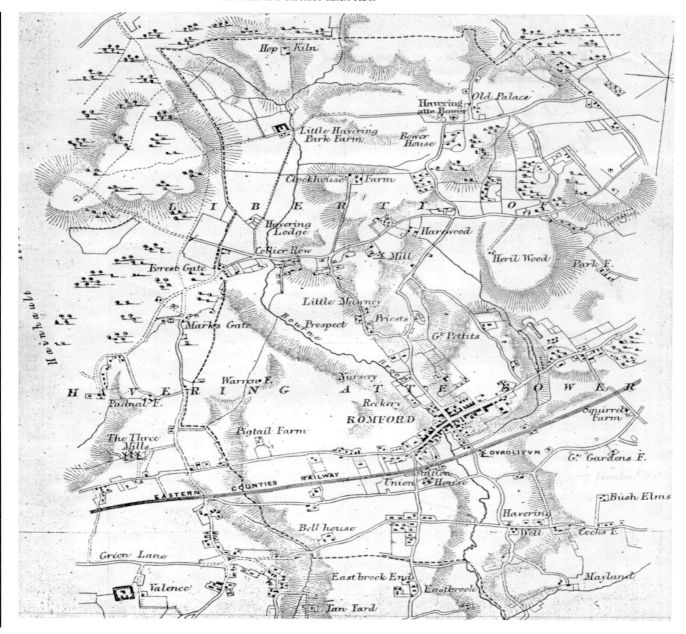

ILLUSTRATIONS.

PAGE.

4	Map of Romford and District circa 1850.
8	Ground Floor Plan of the Workhouse.
15	Wedlakes four horse-power Threshing Machine.
27	Mill for Bruising Oats.
28	Ingrebourne Cottages.
31	Thatched Cottage, Wennington.
41	Hactons.
42	The Cock and Bell Inn.
49	Barking Creek.
50	Transferring the Catch.
61	Three Windmills, Chadwell Heath.
62	Rusty Bacon.
70	Romford Market.
77	Bedstead, Wedlake's Catalogue.
84	Hornchurch, the High Street.
84	Hornchurch, the Corner of North Street.
85	The Bell, Upminster.
85	Cranham Church and Village School.
86	The Brick Kiln.
87	Great Warley.
89	Dagenham High Street.
90	Angling Permits, Dagenham Lake.
92	The Good Intent, Rainham.
111	Five Pound Note from Johnson's Bank
128	The Gatekeeper's Lodge Today.

The author is indebted to the Essex Record Office for permission to use the illustrations on pages 31, 42, 49, 61, 62, 70, and 89.

REFERENCES.

My sources of information have been:-

1. The Minutes of the Romford Board of Guardians, E/RM 1,2,3,4, all beautifully written in copperplate, and redolent with the phraseology of the time. So vividly do its pages convey the spirit of the era that I have deliberately quoted verbatim from it on many occasions.
2. The Victoria County History.
3. The Chelmsford Newspapers of the time.
4. Rural Life of England. William. Howitt. 1844.
5. Havering and Romford. Thomas Bird. E/RO T/P 71.
6. London Labour, London Poor. Henry Mayhew. Vol.2.
7. Relief of the Poor in Havering. 1700 – 1914. Janice Hegarty.
8. Railways in Essex. ERO Seax Series 10. Also ERO Box 105A & B.
9. Pigot's Directory for 1839.
10. White's Directory for 1848.
11. Ye Olde Village of Hornchurch. C. T .Perfect.
12. The Bearblock Farm Book 1835. ERO D/P 115/28/2.

In addition to the above, I am grateful to the Archive Department of the Meteorological Office, Bracknell for details of the weather in the 1830's and '40s; and to Mr. Fred Feather of the Essex Police Museum for information on the policing of Romford.
Most of all, my thanks must go to the staff of the Essex Record Office for their unfailing help and courtesy at all times.

PREFACE.

For thirty four years I worked in the buildings of the Romford Union Workhouse. It had of course long since ceased to be a Workhouse, having been converted into laboratories for the Department of Pathology for Oldchurch Hospital.

No one visiting that cruciform building and its surrounding yards on a daily basis could remain unaware for long of its sombre, forbidding past. Surely, among all buildings, this one would have some tales to tell. I felt too, that there was a strong chance that it would one day be bulldozed to the ground to make room for some more modern excrescence of the ever expanding hospital.

When he came to Romford town, aside from churches, Nicholas Pevsner as I remember it, had comment for only two of the buildings. His remarks on the Town Hall were dismissive, but he was warm in his appraisal of the front façade of the Union Workhouse.

All in all it seemed to me that it would be good thing to write a few notes, and assemble the outlines of its history before, as a building at least, it was lost to the annals of Romford's story. This has turned out to be an engrossing journey of discovery embracing not merely the buildings, but the town also, and all the parishes of the Romford Union, and I hope now that this little volume will in some way catch the imagination of the reader too.

Rather than follow the story in parochial isolation, my aim has been to link this account with the national developments, movements, and legislation of the time, and thus fit it into the context of early Victorian social history.

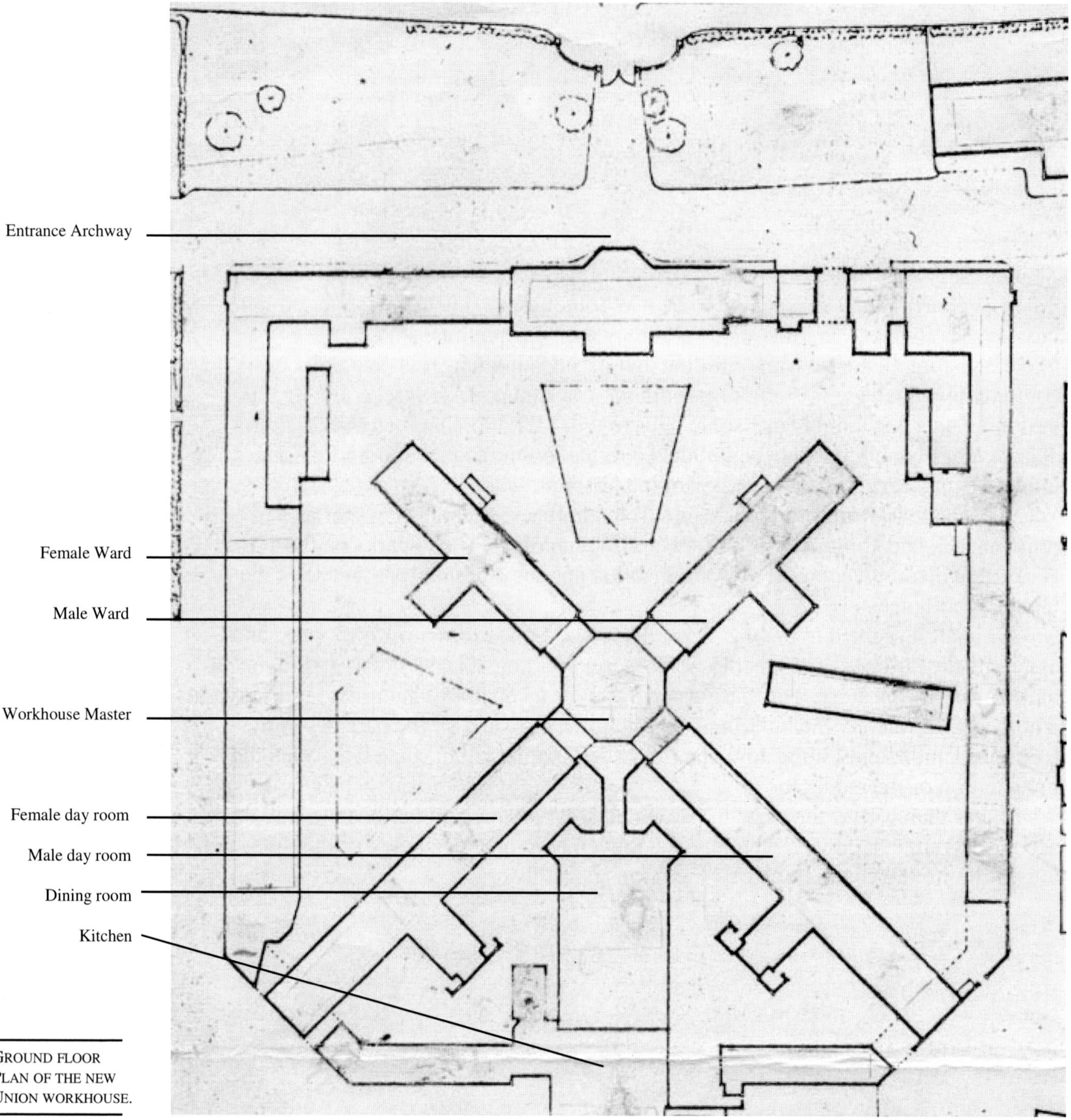

8

Entrance Archway

Female Ward

Male Ward

Workhouse Master

Female day room

Male day room

Dining room

Kitchen

GROUND FLOOR
PLAN OF THE NEW
UNION WORKHOUSE.

1. NEW BROOMS SWEEP CLEAN

The Parishes of the Romford Union.
Essex - No hills, but a bottom of clay.

"28th Dec. 1841: Workhouse accounts for the past 13 weeks examined:
        Provisions for 351 paupers: £759.19.8d, or 5¾d per day.
        Clothing   "   "   "   : £165.4.3d, " 1¼ " " "
        (No mention of any Christmas festivity –not even a
        Christmas dinner.)
        William Mitchell appointed Yardsman (in charge of the
        able bodied men), wages £6 per Quarter plus board
        and lodging with double rations."

This extract from the minutes of the weekly meetings of the Guardians held in the Boardroom at Oldchurch begins to paint a picture of life within the walls of the Workhouse in the winter of 1941-2 . However, to trace the Workhouse's origins, its significance, and its relationship to the surrounding parishes, we must step back in time a further eight years; for this is the story of those ten parishes, brought together by an Act of Parliament.

More correctly, it is the story of eight parishes and two towns clustered together on the Essex bank of the river Thames, and their life and times in the eighteen thirties and forties. The towns were Romford and Barking, and the parishes were their neighbours Rainham, Wennington, Dagenham, Hornchurch, Upminster, Cranham, Great Warley and Havering-atte-Bower. They were of course brought together by the New Poor Law Act of 1834, to form the Romford Union.

25th. Jan. 1842. Quarterly pay day:

Mr. Sellars, Workhouse Master: £16.5.0d
Mrs. Sellars,   "   Mistress £13.5.0d
Miss Pepper, Schoolmistress: £5.0.0d
Mrs. Copsey, Cook:
£2.12.0d
Maria Haseltine, Nurse
£2.12.0d
Rev. Donkin, Chaplin: £25.0
Mr. Griffin, Attorney, Clerk to
        the Board £32.10.

The New Poor Law Act was so called because it was not the first– far from it. The problem of what best to do about the poor ,the aged and infirm, the sick, the hungry and cold, the sufferers of misfortune, as well as those outright scroungers, the workshy 'sturdy beggars', had been us with from Elizabethan times.

England, in her compassion, and with her sense of fairness, had long sought to redress the plight of the poor, and in the early nineteenth century the problem of relieving the poor was becoming increasingly acute. It was not simply the growth of urban populations with the quickening pace of the Industrial Revolution that was exacerbating the situation– though it didn't help.

England was still largely rural, and the parishes of the Romford Union were no exception. Although Romford itself had a population of 4294, and Barking 9036, the eight remaining parishes still had 7191 souls scattered between them, or so we learn from the Census Returns of 1831, and the problem of relieving the poor was primarily a problem of rural England. Each of our parishes had its own, often long established Poor Houses and Almshouses, bequeathed by earlier generations together with endowments for their upkeep, as we shall see.

These were however only part of the story. Able bodied men, many with families, found themselves in utter poverty either because there was no work for them on the land, or even if they were employed, because they were not being paid sufficient for even the barest necessities and food. These men were having to be paid 'Outdoor Relief' by the parish Overseers of the Poor, and their numbers were increasing all the time.

To pay for the Outdoor Relief, Poor Rates were levied on those who were eligible, and in the rural areas these were chiefly farmers, tenant farmers, and copyholders. To keep pace, these rates were going up and up too, and frequently they fell

FROM THE 'OUT OF HOUSE' ABLE BODIED RELIEVED LIST: 4TH. JAN, 1842:-
"Josiah Allsop, 42 years, of Hornchurch; wife and 7 children, wife confined with ninth child: relieved 10 shillings."

unfairly on the smaller farmers, many of whom were being driven out of business only to join the ranks of the unemployed themselves.

Many things contributed to this situation. It would be easy to conclude that National events, Foreign policy, dealings in Government and Parliament, and so on, would be of no consequence to ordinary folk living out their humble lives in the parishes of the Romford Union, yet this was far from the truth. There were four main causes contributing to this crippling rural distress, so evident in southern England.

The first of these was the Napoleonic Wars, which ended with victory at Waterloo in 1815, but whose after effects lived on. During the war prices rose, agriculture boomed and there was inflation. Farmers prospered, often tilling marginal land to increase output. Farmworker's wages rose too, but not enough to keep pace with the price of wheat and hence the price of their daily bread. The price of wheat rose from 58/8d to 94/3d (£2.68 to £4.71) per Quarter between 1793 and 1815. (A Quarter equalled 2 sacks or 4½ cwt.) True, wages in the towns kept up better than in the country, especially for skilled workers, and people did drift off into the towns, and with metropolitan industrial London only a day's walk away, for our folk, the temptation to move must have been strong. On the other hand, the population was rising fast, particularly in the towns, and the end of the war saw over three hundred thousand servicemen precipitously discharged back into civilian life by a Government heavily in debt and anxious to limit that debt as quickly as possible. So there was no easy way out for the rural Worker. Wartime boom was all too quickly followed by widespread slump, with unemployment and falling prices. The Government, struggling to pay the interest on the massive National

It was reckoned that the average working man at this time paid out some 16% of his income on the Duty that was levied on a huge variety of items, from tea to candles, newspaper to glass, beer to cocoa. Income tax was not re-introduced until 1842, and these Duties were a major source of Government income. They fell indiscriminately on rich and poor alike, although it has to be said that Robert Peel had set about reducing and abolishing as many as he could in the interests of freeing up trade.

Debt accrued to pay for the war, kept taxes at a high level. Income Tax, never popular with the landowners and introduced for the first time ever as a wartime expedient, was abolished as promised, in 1816, and this threw an increased burden on the many indirect taxes, (Duties) which fell indiscriminately on the whole community, and thus disproportionately on the poor. With the slump came a fall in the price of wheat. As soon as the war ended it came crashing down from an all time high of 126/6d (£6.33) a Quarter, back to 65/7d (£3.28). The reason? British ports were open once again to imports from France and Europe.

This led directly to the second cause. The Government took fright, and in 1815 Parliament, which overwhelmingly represented the landowners, and naturally acted in their interests, hastily passed the Corn Laws. These stated that no corn was to be imported into Britain until the price of home - grown wheat rose above 80/- a Quarter. This put a floor under the price of wheat to the relief and comfort of the farmer, but to the devastation of his labourers, taking the price of a loaf of bread further out of their reach than ever. This situation applied equally well to the town dwellers of Romford and Barking too.

Compounding these two was a third cause; the weather. Several bad seasons in a row led to poor harvests, and inevitably to further rises in the price of corn.

Finally, there was the solution that went wrong. As far back as 1795 a root and branch attempt had been made to resolve this ever increasing problem of rural poverty; not in the first place in Essex, but in the county of Berkshire. Magistrates met at the Pelican inn in the village of Speen, near Newbury, and they came up with a solution which was to be copied throughout Southern England, and which was to backfire disastrously. They decided to fix the rate of Outdoor Relief according to the price of bread, and to give an allowance according to the size of the applicant's family. In addition, if a farmer paid an insufficient wage, then a supplement would also be paid out of the Poor Rates.

It looked like a reasonable solution, and the system was adopted in county after county. On the positive side, it did guarantee a subsistence wage to the poor, albeit a very low one. But that wage was a fixed one, and worse, the farmers were now being subsidised out of the Poor Rates. What matter if a farmer didn't pay a living wage, Outdoor Relief would make it up! And as for the labourer, what matter if he worked hard all week, or not at all, he still got the same money! The farmer's incentive to pay, and the labourer's incentive to work had been equally destroyed at one go. The entire rural workforce was being pauperised and demoralised. The only way a labourer could increase his income would be to increase the size of his family, or if he was a young man, to get married, and neither of these alternatives was overlooked.

Something had to be done. Local Government, via the good offices of the Lord Lieutenant's magistrates, long versed in administering County affairs, keeping the peace, punishing miscreants, attending to the upkeep of the roads, levying the Poor Rate and overseeing its distribution, had got it wrong this time; fatally wrong.

Now it was the turn of Parliament to step in. At this point we might ask, who indeed was the M.P. for Barking or Romford? The answer is, no one as such! The truth is, that in the elections of 1831 the County of Essex was represented by just three MPs. They were John Tyrell Esq. Of Boreham, Charles Callis Esq. Of Felix Hall, and Arthur Spottiswoode Esq. Who gave his address as Bedford Square. In addition, it should be said, Colchester, population 16,167 returned two M.P.s., as did the town of Harwich, pop. 4010, whilst Maldon, with just 3831 souls, also had its own M.P. It is interesting to note that at this time the population of the whole of the County was 317,507, and that of Chelmsford a mere 5435.

Pressure was beginning to build up on a Parliament which, as already noted, was dominated by landowners from the Shires. Industrialists, especially from the Midlands and the North, were demanding a voice in Government, and in particular for the repeal of the Corn Laws, which they saw as the chief obstacle to Free Trade with Europe and the rest of the world. They wanted easy access to Britain for foreign produce, including corn, in payment for exported British manufactures. Cheap corn also meant cheap food for their factory workers, removing the need for high wages. Cheap food would have helped to alleviate the hardship of the farmworkers in our parishes too.

In addition, even with the French Revolution more than thirty years behind them, Parliament remained preoccupied, not to say terrified that the working classes might rise in emulation of their French counterparts, beheading the king, declaring a Republic, and instituting a 'reign of terror' in the style of their once starving brothers across the Channel. Unrest there certainly was, but did it extend to Upminster, or Rainham, or Romford with its market; or were there mitigating factors?

William Cobbet, the radical who traversed the country preaching dissent against a government so careless of the state of the nation as he saw it, and who published his famous 'Rural Rides' in 1830, seemed to have fairly dashed through Essex on his way to Suffolk and Norfolk. He made only passing reference to the county, but he noted 'There is nothing in Essex (or Suffolk) that can be called a hill'. And again 'Essex, when you get beyond the immediate influence of the gorgings and disgorgings of the Wen (London), that is to say beyond the demand for crude vegetables and repayment in manure, is by no means a fertile county. There appears generally to be a bottom of clay.'

There can be no doubt that the light gravelly soil here on the Essex bank of the Thames, enriched with London's 'night soil', was ideal for good crops of market garden produce. London too, was close enough to supply readily with milk, butter and eggs; and that 'clay bottom' would sustain hefty crops of deep rooted wheat against the dusty days of summer drought. Mixed farming could well have been the established order of things, but even so, with high rents and taxes, and long leases taken out expensively in the war years, profits would be hard to come by, and this in turn kept wages low.

Yet it was mixed farming that saved the day for us. We seemed to escape the worst excesses of the wave of rioting and rick burning that visited the north of the county and Suffolk and Norfolk. The truth is that market gardening and mixed farming offered work pretty well all the year round, whilst further north corn growing predominated, with little work in the winter months particularly now that threshing machines were coming into widespread use, like the one below, pictured in Wedlake's catalogue, literally 4 horsepower, and for sale at 55 to 65 guineas.

THE FOLLOWING ARE EXTRACTS FROM THE BEARBLOCK FARM BOOK (HORNCHURCH HALL) 24TH. OCT.1835:-

Weekly men's wages:		
	Day	14/-d
	Bowdle	14/-d
	Lad	10/-d
	Wells	14/-d
	Basey	14/-d
	Stockley	14/-d
	Rockleff	14/-d
	Humphreys	14/-d
	B. Brett	17/-d
	Smith	5/-d
	Johnson	4/6d
	Boy Wells	4/-d
	" Stockley	3/6d

Nine men were thus employed full time –four on threshing wheat and oats, and four boys – two on crow scaring.
Essex wage rates were above average for the country, but sadly there was still considerable unemployment.

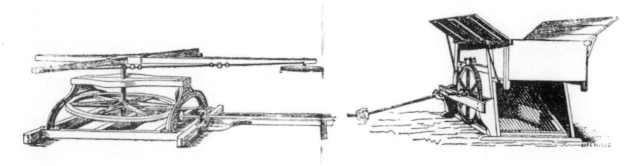

A NEW FOUR-HORSE POWER THRASHING MACHINE.

THE FOLLOWING IS TYPICAL OF THE REPORTS OF THE
ESSEX QUARTER SESSIONS OF THE 1830'S:-

'Puts himself guilty.
Sentenced to be transported beyond the
seas for the term of his natural life to such
place as His Majesty with the advice of his
Privy Council shall think fit to declare and
appoint.
Gabriel Garret, labourer of the parish of
Barking.
For stealing 2 lambs.'

Parochial Poor Law administration had proved itself patchy, ineffective and corrupt, and Government now had to act across the whole breadth of the nation. A Commission was set up under the chairmanship of Edwin Chadwick, which in 1834 published its detailed report with many specific recommendations. To our ears that sounds such a modern thing to do. It was a novel approach then, and it proved to be so effective that it was subsequently adopted for the solution of many other social problems. The Commission's recommendations were accepted and were incorporated into an Act of Parliament, The Poor Law Amendment Act, as it is more properly known.

The Commission, and hence the Law, distinguished between the able-bodied poor on the one hand, and on the other, the old, the frail and the sick, the orphaned poor - such as the all too numerous families of men sentenced by the courts to Transportation, and the lunatics. All these categories were to be no longer handled indiscriminately, as we shall see.
Except as regards medical relief, Outdoor Relief was to be discontinued for the able-bodied and their families. Relief in the form of cash was to be substituted by relief in kind, that is, bread., and the whole administration was to be tightened up.

Parishes were to be grouped together into Unions and responsibility was to be transferred to elected Boards of Guardians for each Union, who in turn would be directed by the Commission, at Somerset House. It is interesting to note that herein lay the very beginnings of the Civil Service. However, individual Parish Vestries were still to be held responsible for levying the Poor Rates and thus meeting the costs of relieving their own poor.

2. THE GUARDIANS ELECTED.

They take the helm.

The Commission directed that the Romford Union could be set up at any time after the 31st. May 1836. No time was lost. The first meeting of 22 elected Guardians, along with a further 9 ex-officio members was held the following Tuesday, 3rd. June, at The White Hart inn, Romford.

These were men of substance, men of standing in the community, anxious to fill their honorary posts.

And who could vote for them in the election? There were sliding scales here:-

Any ratepayer rated for the whole year and paid up, is entitled to vote as follows:-

If he be rated at any sum under £200 - 1 vote.
" " " " " £200 but " £400 - 2 "
" " " " " £400 or more -3 " or,

'Any **owner** *of rated property, provided he gives the address of such rated property in the Union to one of the Overseers on the day previous to the voting is entitled to vote as follows:-'*

If assessed for Poor Rate at less than £50 -1 vote.
" " " " " " £50 to £75 -2 "
" " " " " " £75 " £100 -3 "

And so on, up to £150, or more, entitling him to 6 votes.

At first sight one might conclude that money talks– just another illustration of the class consciousness of Victorian England. However, these people were also the very ones who

The qualifications to stand for election to the Board were quite wide:-
'Any person, not otherwise disqualified by law, who shall be rated to the Poor Rate in any parish in the Union in respect of hereditaments (property) *of the annual value or rental of £20 is qualified to become a candidate for the office of Guardian.'*

would be stumping up the Poor Rates that the Board would be busy spending. There was a sort of rough justice in equating the number of votes with one's likely subscription to this New Poor Law administration.

Five men were returned for Romford, including James Macarthy, chemist and apothecary. His shop was in the market place, and indeed Macarthy's still traded there until 1962. There were eight members for Barking, including George Glenny, who with his brother William, was a market gardener. Another was Thomas Crowe, gent. but remarkably there was no one from the fishing industry.

There were three from Hornchurch, including John Bearblock who was elected vice chairman; two for Dagenham, and one each for Upminster, Cranham, Great Warley, Havering-atte-Bower, Rainham and Wennington.

The member for Havering-atte-Bower was Shadrack Parker, publican of the Cock and Bell, which stood in Romford Market place to the right of St. Edward's church until about 1906. The building later became Church House.

You may think, that with a population twice the size of Romford and returning eight members to the Board of Guardians as opposed to Romford's five, why wasn't it made the 'Barking Union'? Barking certainly thought so, and made strenuous assertions to that end, but the Commission were unmoved. What counted in favour of Romford was its central position, and at a time when you either walked everywhere, or at best rode or drove in a horse drawn carriage, centrality was everything.

Between them, these men were taking over the administration of the relief of the poor, a function hitherto performed by the Justices of the Peace. The implication was that the latter had performed badly, and they were inevitably put out. They would be loathe to yield up the reins; a fact that perhaps shows up in the list of nine ex-officio co-opted members to the Board, for in addition to four clergymen, one a Doctor of Divinity, there were three J.P.s, including Thomas and Octavius Mashiter. The other two members were Major Anderson, gent., of Havering Grange, and William Pearce, gent., whom the Guardians elected to be their chairman.

There was much to be done, and money was going to be at the heart of running the Union. With this in mind, the Board, at its second meeting set about assessing the parishes for the levying of Poor Rates. It based this, not on population but on the average sums each parish had expended on the poor for the years 1833-35, as in the following table:-

SIGNATURE OF THE CHAIRMAN OF THE
FIRST BOARD OF GUARDIANS.

	Av. Expenditure	Call for Funds	(Population)
Romford	£2120	£133	4294
Barking	£4817	£301	9036
Hornchurch	£1855	£116	2186
Dagenham	£1145	£ 72	2118
Upminster	£ 972	£ 50	1033
Rainham	£ 459	£ 29	671
Gt. Warley	£ 302	£ 19	424
Havering	£ 208	£ 13	332
Cranham	£ 145	£ 9	300
Wennington	£ 115	£ 8	127
	£11,958	£750	20,521.

New names applying for Outdoor Relief had to be noted down by the Relieving Officers, or as the Clerk to the Board put it:-
'The names of such persons not being already in the Outdoor Relief list as may apply or be recommended to the Board as proper objects to be placed on the pauper schedules.'

This preliminary call thus amounted to about one fifteenth of the previous year's averages, and warrants were issued for the sums to be paid to the treasurer within fourteen days. Thomas Mashiter had accepted the job of treasurer, having undertaken to give a security of £1000.

Another job requiring early attention was the appointment of Relieving Officers. These would be at the sharp end, listening to and assessing applications for relief. It was decided to appoint two Officers, each at a salary of £80 per annum. One was to cover the First District, which included Barking, Dagenham, Rainham and Wennington, and the other to take charge of Romford, Hornchurch, Upminster, Cranham, and Havering, and Gt. Warley, all of which comprised the Second District.

The Officer would visit each of his parishes in turn, on a weekly basis. His would be the task of divining which were the genuine cases as opposed to the malingerers. He too would have to make the decisions as to who was to be admitted to the Workhouse.

Five candidates presented themselves for interview, and John Benjamin Miller, aged 50 years, was appointed to the First District, with James Parker, 25 years, for the Second District. Each would be handling Union moneys, so each had to give a surety of £60.

A Clerk to the Board of Guardians was also appointed. His name was Edmund Griffiths, attorney, and his salary was fixed at £100 per annum.

There was at this stage no plan to build a single central Workhouse to serve all ten parishes. There was, after all, a large Workhouse in North Street, Romford, and another in North Street Barking. A committee was appointed to inspect all the Workhouses in the Union. Their report recommended that the Romford and Barking Houses only, be retained *'For their*

extent and capabilities to accomplish what is most desirable, namely, a proper classification of the inmates.'
The proposal was that:-

1) All able bodied paupers from 14 to 60 years be supported at Romford Workhouse and divided into three classes, viz. 14 –18 years, 18 - 45 years, and over 45 years. *'The sexes to be kept apart as heretofore.'*

2) The infirm of all ages, as well as persons over 60 years and all children under 14 years, should occupy the Workhouse at Barking, *'The size and capabilities of that Workhouse being so well calculated for the use of the bulk of the paupers of the Union, which the above description of persons will mainly contribute to form.'*

3) All the remaining workhouses to be disposed of to the best advantage and the Overseers of these workhouses were directed to move their paupers to Romford or Barking on Saturday 25th. June 1836, and not to give any Outdoor Relief after Friday 24th. June.

The salary of the Master at Barking was fixed at £50, and the Mistress at £35, p.a., and the Romford salaries were similarly fixed at £45 and £35 respectively.
The Master and Mistress at Barking at that time were Mr. And Mrs. Sellars; and at Romford it was Mr. B.G.Millar, and Mistress Ann Taylor.

Aside from the Commission's intention to make conditions in the Workhouses 'Less eligible', that is, less desirable than those of the lowest paid outside, so as to encourage the inmates to seek work, there was a pressing need to exercise every economy in order to stem the rising tide of Poor Law expenditure.

Every item was scrutinised. Thus it was decided early on to increase the amount of potatoes in what the Board were pleased to call 'The Dietaries', by half a pound per head per day.
'The reason for such increase being that great quantities are

Beer must have at some time been brewed in both the main Workhouses however, because early in January '37 a committee was formed:

'To examine the Workhouses and make the necessary arrangements for the sale of the Coppers and other brewing utensils and to report as to the possibility of disposing of any other fixtures and effects.'

This was duly carried out, for the meeting held on 5th. May noted that:

'Coppers and brewing utensils at Romford and Barking now sold for £103 gross. Mr. Collier's fee for arranging the sale: £18.18.10d.'

grown in the Union, and the people are accustomed to their use.'

Delicately put. The truth was, surely, that spuds were a lot cheaper than bread, even though the bread they bought was made from 'seconds' flour. Not everything was sacrificed to economy however. Dr. Manley, the medical attendant at Barking Workhouse, and a man with a more concerned and caring attitude, as befits his profession, wrote to the Board. His letter requested a *'Daily allowance of beer to the great majority of the paupers at Barking Workhouse on account of their illness, advanced age and general infirmities.'* This made good sense at a time when medicine had little to offer the chronically ill, so the Board directed the beer to be supplied. I imagine the allowance would have been in the order of half a pint a day of 'small beer', which was supplied by Woodfine's brewery in Hornchurch at about £1 a barrel. The better quality table beer, as drunk at the Workhouse Master's table, was 24/6d a barrel (£1.22p).

Strangely enough however, at a meeting on 25th. July,'36, the Board ordered that no milk be allowed for the paupers at Romford or Barking. This was long before the days of pasteurisation –maybe it soured too easily, or was felt to be a health hazard.

Other appointments made at this time were those of the schoolmistress, Anah (sic) Pepper; and the schoolmaster, Mr. Wilding, each at a salary of £20 p.a. Two schoolteachers because as with the other inmates, boys and girls were kept strictly segregated at all times, even if they were from the same families.

Shades of Charles Dickens and Oliver Twist! Sadly Romford Union was to be no exception.

The teachers ate at the Master's table, as did the Porter, Edward Lee, whose pay was £5 p.a. plus *'board and cloathing.'*

Out in the parishes things were moving ahead; men were being actively encouraged to take up work. The minutes of the Board for 19th. July, '36 record, *'A man called Hunt paid £3 by the Relieving Officer for cloathing prior to his going to sea.'* i.e. to join the fishing fleet at Barking.

And again, 13th. Sept., *'The Relieving Officer from the 1st. District to provide cloathing to the amount of £1 each for Joseph Connel and John Taylor to enable them to go to sea, to be charged to Barking Parish.'*

And two weeks after that *'The Relieving Officer at Barking to pay £5 to Thomas Strange, of and belonging to the parish of Barking for apprenticing him to Mr. Thomas, a shoemaker at Woolwich.'*

For all that, Relieving Officers were no soft touch; witness the case of Thomas Everett, aged 22 years, of Hornchurch, granted relief in sickness of 2/-d per week, but *'His illness having arisen from his own misconduct, the advances to be made by way of a loan.'*

Following their closure, it was ordered that the iron bedsteads in the Workhouses at Hornchurch, Dagenham and Upminster be valued and passed to Barking and Romford for the use of the inmates, the parishes to be credited for their value.

These were indeed later valued, and the 14 bedsteads at Upminster were put at £9.16.0d., whilst the ones at Hornchurch were similarly valued, and those from Dagenham came out slightly higher at £11.12.0d.

Ever ready to recoup where they could, and having found it possible to charge the Board rent for their Workhouses, Romford submitted a charge of £100 a year, and Barking one for £200. The Board responded by commissioning Mr. Francis Edwards, of Hart St. Bloomsbury, for a fee of ten guineas (£10.50), to survey them both and to give his opinion on the states of repair and rentals to be paid.

Four weeks later, a deal was struck. Barking agreed to take a rent of £170 p.a. for their Workhouse, *'Reserving to the parish the exclusive use of three rooms now used by the infants school and the girls National School; and the use when it was*

required for parochial purposes of the committee ante –room.'
Similarly, Romford agreed a rent of £85 p.a.

Running the Union was a costly business by the standards
of the day. There was Outdoor Relief, the costs of running the
two Workhouses, and salaries to be paid. Everywhere they
looked, there were calls for money, from £30 a year for the services of a chaplain in each Workhouse, down to paying 5/-d a
week to the barber at Barking, and 2/-d (10p) at Romford.
Assistant Commissioner Wade would come down from London from time to time and help steer the Board, as at the meeting on 4th. October, '36, when the previous quarter's running
costs were examined. These appeared to be £1740.12.2d, made
up as follows:-

Establishment	£230.0.0d.
Out Relief	£775. 8.3d
Barking Workhouse	£551. 19.9d
Romford "	£183. 4.2d.

It was estimated that the running costs for the coming quarter
would be £2521.

Assessment was made on the individual parishes by the
method already described and it was ordered that the sums
were to be paid over to the Union in two equal amounts, on the
first Tuesdays in November and December. The actual costs of
housing inmates in the Workhouses were however apportioned
according to the total number of paupers from each parish, they
being charged pro rata.

The cost per person in terms of clothing food, fuel, maintenance (repairs etc.) per week for Barking were 4/7d (23p), and
for Romford were 10/9d (54p). These figures were to vary con-
siderably as time went by.

Looking for Work.
The Old Parish Workhouses and Selling Them off.

25

3. LOOKING FOR WORK.

The Old Parish Workhouses and Selling Them Off.

It may have been in the minds of the Poor Law Commissioners and members of the Board of Guardians that the implementation of the Act would be a means of bringing the pauper section of the population into line, subjecting them to a little discipline for once, reminding them who was master, and cutting out the mounting waste.

No doubt there was plenty of all this; but there was another aspect too. Amongst the paupers themselves there was for many an increasing realisation that there was light at the end of the tunnel, a way out of past hopelessness and despair.
As already mentioned, paupers could apply for help in seeking work, and the minutes of the Guardian's meetings showed that more and more were doing so. .

A man could arrange for a loan of money for all sorts of reasons. Even before the Union Medical Clubs were up and running, money was being lent out to pay subscriptions to Friendly Societies such as the Forresters and the Oddfellows, whose membership brought insurance against time of need. Thus 3rd. Jan.,'37: *'7/- lent to Thomas Brassing of Barking, to enable him to pay his club, to be repaid at 6d. Per week.'* And *'10/- lent to Thomas Bennett of Dagenham, to be repaid at 6d per week commencing February.'*

Loans were getting bigger too, no doubt for more ambitious projects:-
24th. Jan.,'37: *£1 to William Maler of Barking repayable at 1/-*

'11th. Oct., '36: Henry Aston, an inmate of Romford Workhouse, was allowed to go out Friday and Saturday next to look for work.'
Another entry read:
'10/- lent to James Hodson of Romford to enable him to buy a stock of fish.'
Obviously in this case for setting up in the business of hawking it from door to door.

Loans were made to women too:-
'7th. Feb., '37. 12/- lent to Elizabeth Young of Barking to be repaid at 3/- a quarter.'

It is of interest to note in passing that no mention of any official preparations for Christmas had been made, but now, on 27th. December comes the entry:
'The poor at Barking Workhouse to be allowed to have plum pudding and roast beef on Old Christmas Day, the same to be provided by private subscription.'
Old Christmas Day was 6th. January – the Twelfth Day of Christmas now - and at that time it was celebrated with much merrymaking before the final return to work on Plough Monday.

a week.' and *'15/- each to William Garrett and John Grove of Barking, repayable at 1/- a week.'*
Loans to paupers continued to be made throughout 1837 at the rate of several per week, and Relieving Officers were directed to henceforth take separate account of sums loaned.

We must not forget the older boys in the Workhouse too, and the search for work for them. The minutes of 15th. Nov., '36 note:-
The Master of Barking Workhouse was directed to keep three suits of boys fishing clothing, consisting of:-

1 Fearnought jacket and breeches
1 Pair Sea shoes (Boots?)
1 Southwester
2 Shirts
2 Pairs Sea stockings

For the use of the boys going out on trial as fishermen. Such suits to be returned to the Workhouse in the event of the boys not being bound apprentice.'

And if work was to be the new ethic, then Workhouse inmates were not to be left out, for they were set to productive work from the beginning. Mr. Sellars, Master at Barking, reported receipt of £24. 4 .1d. for wood (splitting logs for firewood?); and Romford House £2.11.8d. for mats and for grinding corn, both in an entry in the Indoor Labour books. Pigs too were fattened on Workhouse swill. At the last Board meeting for 1836 Mr. Sellars was directed to buy 2 pigs for Barking plus 1 for Romford out of the money from the sale of pigs, and to give the balance to the treasurer.
Enigmatically, the minutes of this meeting also included the Item *'Barking, hops sold: £3.8.3d. for the quarter,*
Romford,   "   "   £4.5.1d.   "   "   "
Romford labour: 13/3d.'
Could this have been to do with hop picking on a local farm?

Looking for Work.
The Old Parish Workhouses and Selling Them Off.

27

As for 'grinding corn' in the Romford House, exactly what the workhouse mill amounted to I do not know, but Mr. Wedlake, ironfounder and agricultural implement maker of Hornchurch, attended the Board and undertook to provide a mill for bruising oats for £7, to be put up in a fortnight.

Of course, getting permission to go out of the Workhouse to look for work was one thing; nipping off from church in St. Edwards' on a Sunday was something else - witness the entry in the minutes for 21st. Feb.,'37.;-

'John Riland, Joseph Crouse, and David Simpson absented themselves from church. Also William Smith, Henry Dixon and James Frost. All brought before the Board, who ordered their allowance of meat to be stopped for a fortnight.'

In the Board's eyes, too much meat in the diet was the root cause of all 'ungovernable behaviour'. Or to put it another way, starve them into submission!

Out in the parishes the old torpor of the past was being shaken off too.

Upminster Workhouse, empty now, was sold for £325.4.11d nett, after deduction of the Agent's fees of £21.1.7d, and legal fees of three and a half guineas (£3.13.6d.). The building is there to this day in the form of a row of cottages on the same side as, and just before the Pickled Newt public house, (previously the Bridge House), at the foot of Upminster Hill.

It was built in 1750 on what was described as 'waste land, belonging to Upminster Hall, at the roadside by Ingerbourne footbridge and ford. £110 invested in South Sea Annuities at 4% was cashed to cover the cost of its building. On completion, it cost more than this, but not a lot more. The £4.8.0 interest that the investment would have made, was now made payable out of the parish rates to Mrs. Champion Branfill of Upminster Hall, whose annuities they had been. The interest had anyway been previously used to relieve the poor.

FROM WEDLAKE'S CATALOGUE.

A NEW SYSTEM OF FEEDING HORSES.

OAT CRUSHER, OR BRUISER.

Some thirty years ago, two or three scientific men (surgeons) took into their heads to give their horses oats, only in a crushed state; the result was, that they were much laughed at, and indeed, some of the townsmen of one of them practising at Gravesend, thought the gentleman in question must be insane:—the doctor's horses, however, got into better condition with *a less quantity of corn*, and, notwithstanding the work the animals were doing daily, they got on *better* and were more free from the casualties to which that noble animal is subject.

This machine may be had for hand power at £4 10s. to £6 15s., according to size, and for £13 13s. adapted for horse or water power. The smaller machine will do 2, 3, to 4 bushels an hour ; a quarter, or 2 sacks per day.

This implement is constructed for *the purpose of bruising (not grinding)* grain that is given as food to animals.

Volumes might be written on the *importance* of preparing food for cattle. Several references to coach masters, omnibus proprietors, and scientific persons, who, for these five years and upwards, have adopted that mode of feeding animals. Steam the food you give, or take the kettle and pour hot water on it before giving the food to the animal, who will get on ten times better than he would otherwise.

Once you were off the bottom rung, it was possible to advertise for work:-
From the Chelmsford Chronicle:
*'A lady who has been liberally educated in London wishes to obtain a **situation as governess** in a family in the country; in addition to music and the various branches of an English education she is qualified to instruct in the French and Italian languages, also the rudiments of Latin if required. References of the highest respectability can be given.*

INGREBOURNE COTTAGES - UPMINSTER'S
ORIGINAL WORKHOUSE.

In addition, the Master mended shoes on the premises, and he also taught the children to read and write for a shilling or so a week

Even after it was completed it was still found necessary to board some of the paupers out, so it was extended in 1786. Two years later in 1788, John Smith, the Master was paid 1/9d a week for each of the twenty-eight inmates, plus 2/6d in the £1 of all the pauper's earnings. Although this sum eventually rose to 4/- for each inmate, it remained quite inadequate and the Master had to make ends meet by the labour of the paupers. This involved a risk for the Master, and a harsh incentive to make the inmates work. Among work done at Upminster was oakum picking, growing vegetables in the Workhouse garden ,splitting logs and weaving sacking. Weaving looms were not standard equipment in workhouses, and it was not there from the start. It happened that the Master appointed in 1802 was a weaver from Colchester, and whilst they were interviewing him, the Vestry decided that the inmates should be taught to weave, so he was offered ten guineas to bring down his loom with him, and a shed was put up to house it.

Bread was baked in the Workhouse oven, but as corn got dearer potatoes replaced the bread to a great extent. Meat was eaten when it could be afforded. In 1798 legs and shins of beef were 3d (1.5p) a pound; and double that by 1801. Small beer was drunk, approximately half a pint per inmate each day. Water may initially have come from the river Ingrebourne. Later it was brought down by barrow from a pump at the top of the hill, and in 1818 a well was sunk.

The last Master died in 1835, and his wife Mary Horden carried on until the inmates were moved to Barking the following

Looking for Work.
The Old Parish Workhouses and Selling Them Off

29

year.

It is of interest to note that despite there being 28 inmates, there were only 14 beds on the inventory!

This picture of life in the Upminster Workhouse before the Poor Law Amendment Act, was no doubt mirrored to a greater lesser extent in the Workhouses of the other parishes of the Union.

The Workhouse at Cranham, which was sold at the same time as Upminster's, was both smaller in size and of more recent origin, being less than ten years old at the time of the sale. Always a purely agricultural parish, and thinly populated, what few paupers there were in Cranham had previously been farmed out to South Ockendon.

The building stood at the side of St. Mary's lane, about midway between The Chase (leading up to the church) and Pike lane. Alas, it is no longer there. It sold for just £205, and like the Upminster House it became the property of a Mr. Lowe, who converted both of them into cottages. When it was first erected, it was described as having three rooms downstairs, one of which was used for Vestry meetings. Mr. Lowe converted it into four cottages. One is tempted to ask, did Mr. Lowe build an extension, or did he divide the vestry room into two?

The able-bodied of Cranham, as in the other parishes, were given Outdoor relief, but in 1822 finances must have been getting stretched for the Vestry *'Resolved henceforth to give relief in bread only, other food to be earned by labour.'*

The policy was of course to sell off all the outlying Workhouses. The one at Great Warley had already gone, disposed of back in 1830. It had been built in 1783 and was situated at Headley Common. In its day it could accommodate twenty paupers, but it gradually became unsuitable and run down, and the decision to sell it followed Great Warley's agreement to join with the nine parishes of the Ongar Hundred to set up a

On the other side of the High Street stood another group of almshouses, Appleton's Almshouses, ' *Being let to three poor families who paid 10/2d. A year to the repair fund, they keeping the windows in repair.'*

Workhouse at Stanford Rivers. This it was allowed to do under the permissive i.e. voluntary terms of Gilbert's Act of 1872.

The newly formed Romford Guardians saw it as their job to manage the funds raised by these sales. Accordingly, in 1837 they directed that the £400 standing to the credit of Gt. Warley parish, along with the £325 from Upminster, was to be invested in Exchequer Bonds through Messrs. Johnson and Co.'s Bank. Johnson's was a private bank, issuing its own banknotes as was usual at that time. The senior partner, Thomas Johnson, had taken up the post of Treasurer to the Board following the resignation of Octavius Mashiter from that duty. He had been asked to give his bond of £1000 '*for the due discharge of the duties of his office'*, but being the sharp businessman he was, this he declined to do. On the other hand he offered to take the Workhouse account in the same manner as other customers. Thereupon the Board resolved to open an account with Messrs. Johnson and Co. The day would arrive when they would regret this involvement.

Returning to the sale of Workhouses, Havering-atte-Bower didn't have one, and Hornchurch's wasn't theirs to sell. The best that Havering had been able to do was to rent a five roomed cottage with kitchen from a Mr. Thomas Neave. The practice had been to give out-relief in kind, such as by payment of rent, arranging for medical care, apprenticing orphans, and buying tools of the trade.

The Workhouse at Hornchurch had come into being by enlarging Pennant's Almshouses in 1720. These stood on the corner of Billet lane and High Street, where Sainsbury's is today, and had stood there since they were bequeathed by Pierce Pennant back in 1607. By the beginning of the nineteenth century there were reckoned to be as many as forty inmates, half of them children. It housed the old too. A newspaper cutting of 1835 reads:-'There are at this time in Hornchurch Workhouse 8

Looking for Work.
The Old Parish Workhouses and Selling Them Off.

31

men whose united ages amount to 634 years, also 5 women whose ages amount to 412 years, the youngest of whom is 81 years.'

It remained in use until 1837 when it was converted back into six almshouses, *'Four to be let free, the other two rented to provide a maintenance fund.'* The work paid for by Thomas Mashiter.

As ever, Out-door relief also played its part. From the Overseers and Poor Rate books for Hornchurch :-

1828, Dec. 9. Thos. Biggs, 5 children, petitions for relief of a smock frock for his son, being much distressed for apparel. Granted a smock frock, having a large family of small children.

1829, Nov. 20. Frank Bailey's wife - 4 children - petitions for a pair of shoes for herself. Refused, but allowed a bag of potatoes.

BRICK AND TARRED TIMBER COTTAGES IN WENNINGTON—WERE THESE THE WORKHOUSE COTTAGES?

1831, Dec. 13. John Rich -7 children - applies for a piece of calico for the family and some relief for the children. Granted 8 yards for the children and 2lbs. Bacon, but his character a very drunkard.

Wennington, with a population of only 130 or so, didn't have a proper Workhouse, and as for Rainham parish, their Workhouse was in Wennington!

The Wennington paupers were usually boarded out with neighbouring parishes, but there were two brick and tarred timber cottages with thatched roofs in which they were sometimes housed, or else the cottages were let out and the rents applied to relieve the poor.

Rainham joined forces with Aveley and West Thurrock in 1808, and between them they established a jount Workhouse at Nokehouse, in Wennington. Rainham contributed nine-twentyfifths of the cost of its upkeep, so on the appointed day they had nothing to sell.

The parishioners of Dagenham found themselves in much the same position as Horhchurch. They had converted into a Workhouse a house called 'Wrights' belonging to John Comyn's Charity, and situated in Church Elm lane,'With a baker paid £2 a year to provide bread for widows.' In the 1830's the average number of inmates was reckoned to be about 25, with the men working in the Workhouse gardens, and sometimes put to repairing the roads, their wages subsidised out of the Poor Rate. Before the New Poor Law Act had come into being, Outdoor relief had been on the generous side to help men get back to sea (fishing at Barking), or to become self supporting. Back in the days of the Napoleonic Wars Dagenham had levied a special rate in order to subsidise the sale of bread to the poor. In 1837, on the orders of the Board of Guardians, like those of the other parishes, the paupers were moved to Romford or Barking, and ten years later their erstwhile Workhouse was converted back to Almshouses at the parish expense.

4. MEDICAL OFFICERS AND MEDICAL CLUBS.

With winter approaching, sickness among the paupers was a growing concern and to that end the Clerk was directed to write to the commissioners of the Board's opinion that *'The allowance of bread for breakfast to the paupers in Barking House should be increased from 6 oz to 8 oz for men, and from 5 oz to 7 oz for women and children, the Board feeling that an increase of allowance is absolutely necessary for the health of the inmates, whose conduct has bee uniformly good and worthy of encouragement.'*

General medical care of the paupers had been discussed back in the previous August, when it was decided to divide the Union into seven Districts, each with its own Medical Officer, to be paid according to the size of his District:-

District.	Medical Officer	Salary
1.Romford Workhouse, Romford, Havering, and Dagenham north of the turnpike road.	Mr. Chas. Butter	£50pa.
2.Romford and Dagenham south of the turnpike road.	Mr. Bowers	£40 "
3.Barking including Ripple Ward and the Workhouse.	Dr. Manley	£75 "
4.Great Ilford and Chadwell Wards	Mr. Allison	£50 "

5 Hornchurch, Upminster and pa.	Mr. Quennell	£70
Cranham		
6. Rainham and Wennington.	Mr. Vidal	£20 "
7. Great Warley.	Mr. Cornelius Butter.	£15 "

Midwifery cases to be 10/-d (50p) extra each.

It was a necessary prerequisite of their contracts that all the above Medical Officers should have duly passed the examinations at Apothecaries Hall and Surgeons Hall, or equivalent.

On the whole the system worked smoothly, but there were occasional hiccoughs, such as on 14th. Feb. '37, when Mr. Bowers, M.O. for the 2nd. District was brought before the Board and reprimanded following a complaint that he had failed to attend a pauper of Dagenham by the name of Ellis.

Then there was the case of Mrs. Young, midwife of Romford. She attended the Board and explained *'That she was called in Sunday morning to attend a poor woman living in Sun Yard at Romford, in her confinement; that the woman about and in the morning was delivered of a child, that some time after, finding the case becoming one of difficulty she sent for Mr. Butter, but that gentleman was from home and that she then sent for Mr. Bowers, but that the woman died before he arrived.'* Sun Yard was a notorious group of hovels ranged round three sides of a yard in which filth and offal from a butchery were tipped. It was situated adjacent to the Sun public House, on the main road to Chadwell Heath, just past where Waterloo road is now.

Again, when Mrs. Sellars, Mistress at Barking, attended the Board and explained *'That she had removed Susan Brown a few hours before her death from the ward where other sick persons were, to the nurse's ward adjoining, and that she was*

The report in the minutes of the Board of Guardians called him 'Mr.' Ellis, but then the 'Mr.' was crossed out. Presumably you couldn't be a 'Mr.' and a pauper at the same time.

placed upon a bedstead which was well covered by blankets folded six times under her.' Dr. Manley also stated that he saw the pauper and that *'She had every possible comfort.'*
Could this report have been the consequence of a complaint by a relative of this poor lady?

It is perhaps worth remembering that although there was a nurse, a Mrs. Ling, who was paid 4/-d (20p) a week, most of the work in the Workhouse such as cooking, doing the laundry, scrubbing floors and so on was done by the inmates themselves under the supervision of the Mistress, and this would have included caring for the sick.

Lunatics had to be cared for as well. The Managers of Sir Jonathan Miles Asylum at Hoxton agreed to accept the Union lunatics at 9/-d (45p) a week, and *'The Relieving Officers were directed to have them moved in at the end of the current quarter, moving expenses chargeable to the Asylum Managers.'*

A curious item to our eyes was a tender at this time from Messrs. Sheldrake Briggs and Co., of 29, Leicester Square, for the supply of trusses at 80/- (£4) per dozen, double. The tender was accepted; it clearly met a need, which arose in the following manner –Agricultural produce was sold by the sackful, and a sack of barley weighed two hundredweight, whilst a sack of wheat weighed two and a quarter hundredweights, and a sack of beans was even heavier. Farm workers took pride in lifting these sacks on and off carts, and it wasn't long before they gave themselves an abdominal hernia, or even a double (bilateral) hernia. The days of anaesthetics and antiseptic surgery were not that far away, but they had not yet arrived, certainly for the working man, so the answer was to wear a truss to push the abdominal protuberance back into place.

Three months after the formation of the Romford Union, the Commissioners approached the Board with a view to form-

When paupers died, arrangements had to be made for their burial, and the costs had to be born by the parish from whence they came:-
'No coffins or bearers to be allowed to paupers unless the paupers are buried in the parish in which they happen to die.'

Day to day affairs still clamoured for attention:-
'24th. Jan.'37. Daniel and Thomas Haws admitted to Barking Workhouse, their father Thomas Haws to pay the Relieving Officer 1/-d per week, each.' What tragedy could have overtaken this family?

ing Independent Medical Clubs.

Rather stuffily, the Clerk was directed to write back to say that they didn't deem it expedient to adopt such a system. However, headquarters were adamant, and early in 1837 Assistant Commissioner Wade addressed a meeting of the Board plus the Medical Officers of the Union. Printed copies of the rules under which such clubs would operate were distributed for consideration, together with the following instructional letter:-

RESPECTING THE FORMATION OF INDEPENDENT CLUBS

1. The position of listed paupers is, as has always been the practice ie. The Union will supply free medical aid.
1. Others, not listed paupers, to receive aid, medical or otherwise, as actual necessity indicates. (Sickness in the breadwinner often meant destitution for all the family).
2. Sickness as above is the one in which a labourer would most readily ask for relief, and the one in which the Guardians would find it most difficult to deny. It is a form of relief likely to persist indefinitely and as such cuts across the spirit of the 1834 Act.
3. Alternative provisions for Poor Relief, which strengthen the barrier by which labourers have separated themselves from pauperism must therefore be found.
4. These provisions undoubtedly lie in the formation of Independent Sick Clubs, which are satisfactory alike to the labourers and the Medical Profession. The guiding principles of such clubs are that:-
   a) They should be free of parochial aid.
   b) They should be self supporting.

A month later the Board met again and with the help of Dr. Manley, Mr. Allison, Mr. Vidal, and Charles and Cornelius Butter, finalised a set of rules. These they had printed and circulated in each of the Medical Districts, and the principal rate-payers and farmers were asked for their assistance in obtaining independent subscribers. The rules, which tell us a lot about attitudes and conditions of the time, read as follows:-

1. Members shall be labourers, or in handicrafts and trades, both male and female and strictly of the working classes, but;
    Excluding labourers earning more than £1 per week and domestic servants earning more than £6 per annum.
    (Exclusion may be modified to suit the district).
2. Members on admission shall pay one year's subs in advance, payable on a given date (for all members), preferably in the summer or autumn, ie when most convenient.
3. Members may be admitted at any time on payment of a full current year's subs.
4. Rate for single persons to be   3/- or 4/- or 5/-
    Rate " Married couples   4/- " 5/- " 6/-
    Rate " Couples + 1 child   5/- " 6/6 " 7/6
    Rate " Couples + 3   "   7/- " 8/3 " 9/-
    Rate " Couples + 4   "   7/9 " 9/- " 10/-
    Rate " Couples + 5   "   8/6 " 10/- "11/-

    On payment they shall be entitled to all requisite advice and medicine from the Medical Officer of their choice.
    (I expect the individual M.O.s fixed the actual pay scale for their district.)
5. Children over 16 years to count as single persons unless idiots or permanently crippled.
6. The wife of a member may be attended in her confinement on payment of 5/- or 7/6d or 10/6d to the M.O. before confinement.

Of course, if you had a few coppers to spare, there was always patent medicines, advertised with their usual modesty
This, from The Chelmsford Chronicle of the times:-

C.S. Chedden's Famed Herbal Tonic Pills.

For the cure of Scrofula, Scurvy, Scorbutic affections, Eruptions and pimples on the face and other parts of the body, Swellings or ulcerations of the neck, Sore breasts and all disorders attended with painful swellings, Morbid and irritating eruptions of the skin, Open wounds and sores, Contraction of the limbs, Enlargement of the joints or glands, Lameness, Morbid secretions, General debility, Nervous affections, Lumbago, Loss of appetite, Indigestion, or where the constitution has been injured by excesses, Diseases of any kind, Mercury or any other injudicious treatment, and in all those cases in which Sarsaparilla or tonics are of no avail, these pills have proved far superior to any other medicine.(!)

Sold by Meggy and Chalk, Chelmsford, in boxes at 1/1½d, 2/9d, 4/6d, and 11/- each.

7. A man and his wife may subscribe for themselves alone, or for their children alone, but not for a single child separately.

8. Aged and infirm parents may be subscribed for, if resident with the member, and counting as children under 16 years,

9. Nobody who is actually ill can join, save that 2 healthy persons join at the same time, or unless they pay an extra fee to be arranged with the M.O., but in subsequent years the fee to revert to normal.

10. The M.O. of choice to be indicated at the time of paying subs. And no change allowed until the next payment.

11. Sick members to supply own bottles and bandages, and in case of rupture, own trusses; and when possible to go to the M.O. The M.O. to visit them only when unable to attend.

12. Drunkards etc. idle and disorderly persons, persons convicted of a felony, not to be allowed to join.

13. Respectable persons to be appointed stewards of the Club. They shall collect subs. and be the final arbiters in all disagreements within the Club, which latter must be brought before them.

14. Name, age, and address must be registered of each member on payment of subs. And this registration to be renewed annually with each payment.

15. Subscriptions to be paid on the day due. Members out of benefit if not paid up within 14 days. Upon payment of a fine of say 6d. They may be re-admitted to the Club

16. The stewards to pay the subscriptions to the M.O.s indicated by members at once.

The clubs flourished, and for the people in our ten parishes, this was a giant step forward, reflecting the growing spirit of self-help which was to be so characteristic of the unfolding Victorian era.

Alongside this came another development. The Government passed the Marriage Act, and this allowed, for the first time, for Catholic and Dissenting Protestants (Wesleyans and Methodists) to be married by their own ministers, instead of as hitherto, by a Church of England parson only.

The proviso was such that marriages, and C. of E. ceremonies too for that matter, should henceforth be notified to a Registrar. Thus was created the new post of Registrar, who in effect took over the keeping of the parish registers.

All marriages, as well as births and deaths would now have to be reported to him, and for a fee he would issue the appropriate certificate.

For the Government this was a new and useful source of statistics to put together with the ten year Census Returns. For the Board of Guardians, it was another item to organise! The two Relieving Officers were given the responsibility of fixing printed notices – supplied by the Registrar General- to church and chapel doors, and other conspicuous buildings, advising the public of the change.

Four Registrars Districts were set up:-

1. Romford: Romford,Havering and Dagenham.
2. Hornchurch: Hornchurch, Upminster, Cranham, Rainham, Wennington and Gt. Warley.
3. Barking: Barking town and Ripple Wards
4. Great Ilford: Great Ilford and Chadwell Wards.

For each District a Registrar was appointed, they being Mr. Bowers for Romford, Mr. Quennell for Hornchurch, Dr. Manley for Barking, and Mr. Allison for Ilford, all of whom already held posts as Medical Officers.

Medical Clubs were a good investment from the start, even if you couldn't find the subs. immediately:-

'23rd. May,'37: 11/-d lent to William Barker of Barking to enable him to join the Medical Club. To be repaid at 6d. Per week.'

Many such loans were made at this time.

Further, as part of the parish church living, an acreage of Glebe land was often included, as at Great Warley, where the living was described as:-'*A good residence and fourteen acres of Glebe,*' or Cranham, where the Glebe ran to forty acres.
A parson could farm, and sometimes did.

The Clerk to the Board, Edmund Griffin, accepted the post of Superintendent Registrar.

For the time being it was decided to defer setting up a permanent office, but to provide a room in the Romford Workhouse instead, with an iron chest for the safe keeping of documents and registers.

The Poor Law Amendment Act, with its Workhouses and Boards of Guardians; the setting up of Medical Clubs for the working classes; and now the Marriage Act liberalising the wedding ceremony and instituting the registration of births marriages and deaths, all within the space of a couple of years, brought changes that touched upon the everyday lives of every parishioner in the Romford Union. Things were beginning to move, and fast.

Yet another Act, the Tithe Commutation Act, affected this time the farmers and the clergy.

The Church could demand the payment of tithes in the form of every tenth sheaf of corn, every tenth piglet, every tenth calf, and this had long been a source of contention with farmers, for it was they, and not the landowners who paid.

But now, with the passing of the Act, all tithes were commuted to payment in cash. Detailed maps of each parish were prepared, and every field was assessed for tithe payment, and thus the farmer's dues were fixed for all time, and varied no more with the size of the harvest.

Further reform was brought upon the Clergy by another Act, this time designed to do away with the worst excesses of the unequal distribution of wealth within the Church.

Plurality, by which one parson could cover a number of parishes and hence command the income from their livings, plus the tithes, was to be restricted by law; and the cathedral clergy, hideously overpaid, were to be reduced in numbers and wealth. The money saved by this Act was to be redistributed among the poor clergy.

It should be noted in passing however, that a considerable part of the tithes may well have been sold off by now to a layman 'impropriator', leaving only a lesser portion for the parson.

Within the ten parishes of the Union the average value of a living was about £450 a year, which together with the gross tithes before impropriation averaging another £490, made up a very comfortable income.

Among our clergy, the vicar of St. Edwards, Romford, the venerable Anthony Grant D.C.L. was also Archdeacon of St. Albans, so he may well have seen a reduction in his income.

There was too, the case of the reverend R. Battiscombe. His address was given as Hacton House, on the borders of Upminster, but he officiated for the rector of Wennington, one reverend George William Curtis. This would have put him in the position of curate to the rev. Curtis, and thus in his pay. Curates were notoriously poorly paid – often poorer than their own church mice. On investigation however, it turns out that the rev. Battiscombe was no poor curate. The truth was that he actually owned Hacton House, having bought it in 1841. A most elegant residence, it had been built back in 1765 by William Braund, a retired City Financier, and it still stands today, at the junction of Gaynes Park road and Hacton lane, and now converted to flats.

HACTONS

So, for a poor curate we must turn to Havering-atte-Bower. The living of the church of St. John the Evangelist was said to be very poor, and the vicar in the 1820's and '30's, the reverend Henry Ward, rarely resided, but employed an assistant curate. This turns out to have been a man called James Wiseman, who was also a local farmer. What he got for his troubles, heaven alone knows, and whether he benefited from the redistribution of clerical wealth, I hesitate to say.

'THE COCK AND BELL' ROMFORD, WHERE
SHADRACK PARKER WAS PUBLICAN.

One Workhouse or Two?
Barking the Fishing Town; Ilford the Staging Post.
Child Labour and Education.

43

5. ONE WORKHOUSE OR TWO?

Barking the fishing town; Ilford the staging post.
Child labour and education.

From the outset, the Commissioners at Somerset House had wanted the Board of Guardians to go for a single Workhouse. The Board were equally adamant that there was no need for such extravagance; the Houses at Romford and Barking could be made to do the job. In spite of the attendance of Assistant Commissioner Wade at a special meeting held on Saturday 18th. Feb.,'37, the Board stuck to their guns. After all, both Houses had been purpose built, and were quite large – big enough to hold 250 inmates apiece.

They had been completed within a year of each other, Barking's in 1788 at a cost in excess of £4000, had a central two storeyed block with two wings, together with a basement and a factory for making sacks. (They never made a success of the factory, despite several attempts.) The money for the building had been raised on loan, and as late as 1813, £4254 was still outstanding.

Romford's Workhouse stood in North Street, on the left, just before Como Street. It cost £3500 to build, and had been erected by Messrs. Abraham Godden and Richard Moore, bricklayers (builders) in the town. As a building, it was widely quoted as a 'model Workhouse'.

Each was the result of its own separate Workhouse Act of 1776, by which Acts, responsibility for the poor of each town was transferred to a new body to be called The Directors and Guardians of the Poor. Unlike the present Guardians, the six members of these two new bodies were not elected, but co-opted from among persons rated at £200 a year or more, plus the vicar. They were separate and distinct from the old Vestries, and were empowered to do such things as appoint salaried Workhouse Masters and Mistresses.

Now, in 1837, they had in turn been superseded by a single, much larger, elected body; the Board of Guardians, and if the Board were to get its way it would be only if they agreed to the Commission's request to *'Put the Houses in a condition to admit of the complete application of the Workhouse Regulations.'* Assistant Commissioner Wade suggested that the proper plans and estimates be forwarded to Somerset House for that purpose.

One might ask, what in Commissioner Wade's eyes, was so wrong with these Houses? Well, for a start, they were both fifty years old and in need of running repairs, as a list of the Romford bills at the end of March '37 shows;-

King.	Plumber.	£24.6.9d.
Holmes.	Bricklayer	£10.13.10d
Spicer.	Blacksmith.	£4.17.6d
Dangerfield.	Carpenter.	£11.18.3d.
Wedlake.	Stoves.	£17.18.3d.
Bartlett.	Repairs.	£9.19.8d.

In July, '37., a tender was accepted for the repair of plaster, wash, stop, colour and lime white the Workhouse at Barking for £9. A year later, the same man, our Mr. Holmes the bricklayer, put in another tender for decorating Barking Workhouse, this time for £15. It too was accepted.

Again, Mr. Butters, Medical Officer at Romford Workhouse, submitted a report on the state of the House, requesting:-

1.   The two yards be re-gravelled. (12 loads used).

Also mentioned at this time was the business of the infirmary in Romford's Workhouse, in which a committee of Guardians was appointed :-
'To find some plan for preventing all communication between the sexes(!).'

One Workhouse or Two?
Barking the Fishing Town: Ilford the Staging Post.
Child Labour and Education.

45

2. Twelve bowls and towels of coarse linen be provided, and the men and women wash thoroughly every morning before breakfast
3. That the yarn room be cleaned and whitewashed immediately; Mr. Butter to fix the number of men employed therin.
4. That the rooms and passages be immediately cleaned and whitewashed.
5. That a stove with a thermometer regulator be fixed immediately in the men's dayroom. (This was midwinter, Feb.,'38)

There was duplication too. This ranged from items like insurance:-

Barking furniture: with Royal Exchange Assurance: £10.1.6d.
Romford   "   "   Sun Fire Office.   : £4.9.0d.
right through to the salaries for two Masters and two Mistresses, not to mention lesser lights such as Porters and Nurses.

Still confident in the rightness of their decision, the Board proceeded to get estimates for the necessary upgrading. Francis Edwards was appointed surveyor, and a month later he duly submitted his plans and estimates. They came as a nasty shock, hugely exceeding the Board's guestimates. Mr. Bearblock, the Chairman, suggested they abandon the idea and call a special meeting forthwith to consider replacing them with a new central Workhouse.

Mr. Mashiter steadied things up; he proposed they go through the estimates closely, which they did, and by the end of the meeting he had won his fellow members over for the now approved figures to be forwarded to the Commissioners.

A month later and Assistant Commissioner Wade attended again to hear the Board re-affirm their belief that the two Workhouses should continue and that the (expensive) repairs

The earlier decision to do without milk
must at some time have been reversed,
witness the accounts;-
27th. June, '37.
Milk for Barking: *£3.3.4d.*
"   "   "   :   7/-d.
At 8d. per gallon, this represents 95 gals.
for Barking, or just about eight pints a
day for the whole of the Workhouse's
needs!

required *'For the complete classification of the inmates'* be taken in hand without delay.

Meanwhile, the run of the mill weekly affairs of the Board, such as paying staff, paying Union Medical Officers, accepting tenders for the supply of the two Houses, and so on, continued, interrupted only by the following scandal:-

It appeared that a Mr. Samuel Brown of New Norfolk Street Islington, attended the Board stating that his mother, Ann Brown, who was admitted to Barking in a state of exhaustion and destitution on 7th. August on the order of Mr. Miller, Relieving Officer, had taken with her, from him, a purse containing 26 sovereigns and 3 half sovereigns. The morning after admission the money in her pocket was found to be 16 sovereigns only, with 5 half sovereigns, a five shilling piece, two half crowns, and six shillings and sixpence in silver.
The Board entered into a lengthy examination of the persons who had attended Ann Brown, and particularly Eleanor Gates, and Mary Lucas (neither of whom were in the employ of the Guardians, and must have been fellow inmates), when it appeared that the latter had been seen to take a quantity of gold out of the pocket, and to count it. A careful search was made and the ten sovereigns were found by the Matron in a box belonging to Mary Lucas, who was thereupon committed by Mr. Pearce for examination before the Justices at Ilford on Saturday next on a charge of stealing the money.

At the next meeting the Board, being satisfied that Samuel Brown was well able to support his mother, it was directed that notice be given to him to take her out of the Workhouse, and that in the meantime he will be held responsible for the expenses of her maintenance. The board further directed that the prosecution of Mary Lucas be conducted at the expense of the Union, and charged to the establishment.
Whereupon Samuel Brown attended again and claimed the

One Workhouse or Two.
Barking the Fishing Town: Ilford the Staging Post.
Child Labour and Education.

47

£27.10.0d which he alleged had been stolen from him by his mother. He pointed out that he had not the means of properly looking after his mother, so the Board agreed to her staying in Barking House if he contributed 1/6d per week towards her keep. He then paid £2.1.6d, which together with the silver to the value of £1.16.6d that had been found on her, made up a year's contributions. In the event of her death it was agreed that a proportionate sum be returned to him.

What a joy, to have a son so full of filial care!

Back to the fate of the Workhouses. A letter from the Commissioners arrived authorising the necessary alterations; this was signed in turn by all the Guardians, as was required. They had been right; their decisions vindicated, or so it must have seemed, when eleven weeks later to the day a further letter arrived, this time from the high priest, Edwin Chadwick himself. It said that the Commissioners had decided with regret that it was their duty to withhold sanction from the proposed Workhouse arrangements.

Chadwick, the man whom Parliament had instructed to compile the far reaching and detailed report upon which the Poor Law Amendment Act had been based, and who had been given the job of heading the triumvirate of Commissioners to oversee its implementation, had finally got his way.

There was after all, to be just one Workhouse to serve the Romford Union.

To their credit, our men took it in their stride. At the very same meeting they decided to investigate the possibility of obtaining land adjoining the Romford House, so as to extend it sufficiently to answer all the purposes of the Union.

As a result of this ruling, Barking was now going to be without a Workhouse; no doubt to the surprise of those of its 9,000 citizens who took an interest in civic affairs.

The fate of Mary Lucas I have been unable to ascertain. Suffice it to say that men were transported to Australia for far less.

ADVERTISEMENT FROM THE FRONT PAGE OF
THE CHELMSFORD CHRONICLE, FRIDAY,
MARCH 13TH, 1835:-

" HIGHLY VALUABLE ESTATES.

To be sold by auction by T. Harvey.

*On Tuesday March 24th. 1835, at One
O'clock, at The Bull Inn, Barking. Essex
by order of the executers of the late Mr.
John Brown, deceased, comprising;-*

*Six highly valuable Dwelling Houses,
with extensive Store Warehouses and
Lofts, Large Wharf, Garden and Premises, situate abutting upon Mainbridge
or Fisher Street, Barking, Essex.*
*The Property may be viewed by applica-
tion to the tenants, and particulars had,
seven days preceding the Sale at Inns at
Barking, and of T. Harvey, Auctioneer,
Estate Agent &c., Ilford, Essex."*

*' The fishery is a nursery of a hardy in-
dustrious race, who seldom fail to become excellent sailors.'*
Her Majesty's Navy certainly thought
so, for Barking was a fertile ground for
the Press Gangs.

In the second quarter of the nineteenth century. The town was above all a fishing port. We have seen how the Relieving Officers of Dagenham and Romford and Rainham were ever ready to materially help men to get back to sea; how Workhouse Masters were instructed to keep suits of clothes ready for boys to be apprenticed to the fishing.

Situated on the banks of the river Roding, some two miles from its confluence with the Thames, Barking was the prime supplier of fresh fish to Billingsgate and the sprawling city of London.

According to Pigot's Directory for 1839, as many as 1200 men and boys were employed in the industry. It was something of a boom town; the old Barking Directors and Guardians of the Poor admitted freely that but for the fishing continually taking on labour, their problems would have been much more acute.

In 1833 there were 120 fishing smacks putting to sea, and by 1850 this number had gone up to 220, each with a crew of eight, half of them apprentices. The local seamen were said to be less than average height, a fact that they believed made it more difficult for them to be washed overboard in rough weather!

The boats, displacing some 40 to 60 tons, put out to fish as far away as the coasts of Holland and Scotland for turbot and sole and cod, which was stored live below decks in wooden wells filled with sea water, pending return to port. 61 Smack owners are listed in the pages of Pigot, many sharing family names like the Forges; with John William, and Thomas, and Richard, and Richard junior; and the Harris's, with Sarah, and John, and Joseph and Thomas junior, all separately listed; and Jacob and Christopher Spashett.

One man, Samuel Hewett, the son of a Scottish fisherman, Scrymgeour Hewett, and the owner of some sixty smacks himself, revolutionised the fishing. He organised the boats into a

One Workhouse or Two?
Barking the Fishing Town, Ilford the Staging Post.
Child Labour and Education.

49

BARKING CREEK.

single outfit under the banner of 'The Short Blue Fleet'. It was he who introduced cutters into the fleet. These were larger than the sturdy smacks, and very fast – the fastest boats afloat when having to beat upwind. Each day the smacks would transfer their catch, in boxes now, instead of the old cran baskets, to the cutter which would return to Barking with its cargo; thus allowing the smacks to stay on the fishing grounds for longer.

He it was too, who began the use of ice on the boats. Low lying land was flooded in the wintertime, and when it froze over it was cut into blocks and carted off to straw-lined ice-houses to be stored until it was required.

Most years, the first cartloads would come clattering through the town on or about the 16th. November, a signal to the people

In 1865, Robert, son of Sam Hewett moved his trawlers to Yarmouth. The extension of the railway (see chapter 9) to the East Coast ports thus led to the collapse of Barking as a fishing port.

John Moore (1820–1902)
Signed and dated 1884

Transferring the Catch
Oil on canvas 12″ × 18″

THIS PICTURE DEPICTS HEWITT'S SHORT BLUE FLEET DURING FISHING OPERATIONS OFF THE DOGGER BANK IN HEAVY WEATHER.

of Barking that winter had arrived.

The town itself, with its wharf and basin and toll-free quay, was a tight, overcrowded little place, busy making and selling boats, and sails and spars and ships chandlery. The noise of caulking hammers filled the air.

It must have stood in sharp contrast to East Ham, its neighbour across the Roding. The people of that town today will be amused to learn that early Victorian times it was described as

One Workhouse or Two?
Barking the Fishing Town: Ilford the Staging Post.
Child Labour and Education.

51

*'The residence of many opulent families; from this neighbour-
hood the views over the opposite shore of Kent are exceedingly
picturesque.'*

The odour of fish being carted to Billingsgate was not the
only smell to assail Barking noses. The quayside was a convenient place to offload barges of London's 'nightsoil', brought
down the Thames to fertilise the prolific fields inland to the
north, around Ilford and Chadwell Street. The northcountry
saying 'Where there's muck there's brass' could just as well
have been coined in Barking.

One way or another, muck there was aplenty. The town houses
were in low, close alleys in which diseases like cholera could
spread quickly. Drainage was bad, pigs roamed the streets.

The Vestry were not much concerned to do anything about
it, but some of the residents thought otherwise, and in 1846 a
committee was formed to investigate drainage and refuse dis-
posal. Even then, only limited action was taken.

And as for the 'nightsoil', Henry Mayhew in his book
'London Labour, London Poor', gives a detailed account of its
preparation from the City's cesspits, which were emptied by
hand, on average just once a year. When first collected it was
tipped into lagoons in the East End, and left to drain. It was
then stacked to dry out further before being mixed with spent
hops and stable manure rich in straw, and finally bagged, ready
for delivery to the farms. Judging by the frequent complaints
from Barking's long suffering inhabitants, even after all this
treatment it still smelled to high heaven.

It was not all doom and gloom however. There was some
light at the end of the road, literally, for the Gas Works, opened
in 1836, was producing gas now, to light the streets of Barking.

Ilford too, had its Gas Works, situated on an island in the
Roding and opened in 1839. These were privately owned

Water was supplied solely from wells and pumps, and Ilford's inhabitants needs were handsomely met by a reported

'A never failing public well.'

works, set up no doubt in response to the lately passed Lighting and Paving Act. Although it was made a separate parish eclesiastically in 1830, Ilford was, along with Ripple Ward and Chadwell Ward, still in civic terms part of Barking; and together they represented the other arm of Barking's prosperity. What with the grazing of beef along the marshes, for which very good premiums were paid, and potatoes and market gardening to supply London, much intensive farming was in evidence. Besides 600 acres of potatoes and 150 acres of cabbages; onions, turnips, asparagus, apples, plums, currants and walnuts were all sent to market, to say nothing of corn. Barking and Ripple, together with Ilford and Chadwell Wards had 5,700 acres of arable farmland plus 3,600 acres of pasture, as well as 1,600 acres of Hainault forest within its boundaries.

Yet even with the rural hamlets of Barkingside to the north and Chadwell Street to the west, Ilford wasn't simply agriculture. The place had come into being, at this point where the turnpike road crossed the river Roding and where the crossroads led down to Barking in one direction and to Wanstead and Walthamstow in the other, and it filled a need.

Fifty or sixty or more coaches a day would pass along the turnpike road, this main artery connecting London with East Anglia right up to Norwich, to say nothing of the wagon loads of goods and produce bound for London. There were many inns and coaching houses catering for travellers; horses would be in demand, and stabling to manage them; and a complement of shops and traders for the inhabitants themselves. It was a Staging Post.

Only the sturdiest thirteen and fourteen year old boys were sent off to serve out their apprenticeships on the fishing smacks, but that wasn't to say that the rest languished at home doing little jobs for mummy. In the 1830's and '40's most children would be employed from time to time. Out on the farms

One Workhous or Two?
Barking the Fishing Town; Ilford the Staging Post.
Child Labour and Education.

53

there was weeding, picking stones (used to repair the roads), and pea picking and gleaning in season. And even if you did stay at home, you minded the house and the young ones, in charge because mum herself was out daylong working in the fields to supplement the family's meagre income.

Children were often organised into gangs by the farmer, and put to work in the fields under a master. Boys were employed at scaring birds off the growing crops too, but farmers took good care to keep them well apart lest they lose sight of the job on hand and turn to sporting among themselves Conditions were harsh and the pay miserably low. Girls as young as ten would be put out to Service– if they were lucky, to somewhere local in the first place, that they might return home at weekends to see their brothers and sisters.

There was a saying among farmers. *'One boy is a boy, two boys is half a boy, and three boys is no boy at all!'*

But changes were on the way. The Nation's conscience awakened and appalled at the brutality of women and children having to work down the coalmines ,and at the long dreary hours of the children working in the cotton mills of the North, was turning its attention belatedly to the question of education for the young.

In 1833, for the first time, Government made provision towards education, a modest £20,000 a year for schools. There was at this time no compulsion for children to go to school at all. As we have seen, the need to go and earn vital pennies to bolster the family's slender purse too often overrode all else.

There were schools of course, quite an assortment of them, from Dame's schools to Boarding Academies, and Barking and Ilford had their share.

Among the foundations of any consequence, Ilford had the Cricklewood school. Originally under the wing of the Barking Church School Committee, it had joined forces with the National Society (part of the Anglican church) for funds, before being taken over by the Ilford Education Committee in 1837.

Nine years later, Nancy and Eleanor Thompson, of the Clements Estate, built an infants department, and in 1842 a Church school was built at Barkingside.

For Barking town there was the Free Grammar School, as it was originally called. Back in 1776 the then newly created Directors of the Poor had taken it over. It consisted of two large buildings, one, the master's house; and there was an endowment of £20 a year which paid the master's salary. Part of this site was used to erect the town Workhouse, and in 1778 the school was re-opened for 20 boys and 20 girls aged 7 to 11 years. The boys were taught the three R's, and the girls reading writing and 'home spun work'. 'Only minimum corporal punishment was permitted, and the children to be given a dinner in the Workhouse'. In 1792 the Master was allowed to take 12 private pupils, and to hold an evening class for girls.

In 1810 the Local Education Committee re-organised the school, raised funds to provide more places, and augmented the teachers salaries. From then until 1836, the school was run by Oliver Lodge, the parish lecturer, and under him the number of pupils rose from 40 to nearly 400, with the master's salary at £37 a year, and the Mistress £30 a year. It too, joined forces with the National Society, and in 1827 a new building was erected in the Workhouse garden, which became the boys school. Finally, in 1845 a Wesleyan School was opened.

Government funding for education rose rapidly, and Inspectors of Schools were appointed to see that the money was not wasted. Progress however, remained slow, with few new schools being built; and the low pay for teachers failed to attract any but the least qualified. It was to be another forty years before schooling was free and compulsory to the age of ten, but a start had been made.

Buying the Land, Choosing the Builder.
Chadwell Heath's Three Windmills.
Romford and the Market; its Businesses and Shops.

55

6. BUYING THE LAND, CHOOSING THE BUILDER.

Chadwell Heath's Three Windmills.
Romford and the Market; its Businesses and Shops.

Travelling along the turnpike from Ilford, a short journey of some five or six miles would take us through Chadwell Street, across Chadwell Heath and back to Romford town.
Chadwell Heath was a heath, gorse ridden and rough. It was inhabited mainly by gypsies, who scraped a living by lopping, and grazing assorted animals. People felt easier when they reached the far side. At Chadwell Heath too, there were no less than three windmills, standing together, just back from the road. All three were post mills, one going back to 1770, the other two built in 1810 and all owned by Archer Moss, whose family carried on milling right through to the outbreak of World War 1. One windmill was a business, three showed entrepreneurial flair, especially by the side of the turnpike with its ready access – easy for sacks of corn in, easy for sacks of flour out.

Back in Romford again, we must turn our attention first to Workhouse matters, and to those civic stalwarts, the Board of Guardians, anxious now to get about building a new House. They soon discarded the idea of simply extending the North Street House. Three surveyor/architects, Messrs. Edwards, Kempthorne, and Savage, when called in by the Board gave as their opinion that *'It would be highly inexpedient to build an entirely new House on the present site even if additional adjoining land were available; if more eligible land can be obtained within one mile of Romford.'*

TURNPIKE TRAFFIC A TEMPTATION TO THIEVES: EXTRACT FROM THE CHELMSFORD CHRONICLE :-

'Brentwood and Warley Gang.
The following were fully committed by W. Davis Esq. to the gaol at Ilford for trial at the next Quarter Sessions;- A Ballard, J. Shrimpton, F. Mingey, and J. Cracknell, charged with robbing Hewitt & Co's Colchester wagon whilst stopping at the White Hart Brentwood on Saturday night the 7th. Inst., and —Turvey and A. Ballard charged with receiving articles stolen , with a knowledge of such.
Two of these men were apprehended by Weston, the Bow Street patrol stationed at Romford, in a wood near Thorndon Hall. It appears that one of the men had taken a house at Brook Street to open as a shop to be supplied with goods by a brother who resides in London.' (?Hopeful alibi).

There was a brisk trade in farms and land throughout Essex anyway:-

Cheese Cross, Romford.
TO BE PEREMPTORILY SOLD BY AUCTION.
by S. Collier.
On the premises on Friday August 16, at two o'clock, by direction of Mr. John Tyler, jun. who is about to move to Devon. 54 Acres of luxuriant growing crops of corn, two stacks of meadow hay and the unexpired term of three years tenancy of the farm.

LAND AND COTTAGES AT HORNCHURCH.
SHUTTLEWORTH & SONS are instructed to sell by auction at the Auction Mart on Tuesday 13th. August at twelve, in two lots, a copyhold estate, situated in the parish of Hornchurch consisting of seven acres of arable, let at a rent of £16 p.a. Also two freehold cottages with gardens situated on Butts Green, and let at rents amounting to £12 p.a.
Particulars and conditions of sale had at The White Hart Romford, The Bell, Upminster, and at the Auction Mart, 18, Poultry.

Potential sites were offered without delay. No doubt certain landowners saw this as an opportunity to sell a parcel of land at a very advantageous price. The offers included:-
Apiece of land near the eleventh milestone on the London Road, belonging to Mr. Orbell.
Land adjoining the road leading from Havering Well to Rush Green, belonging to Thomas Mashiter.
Two more pieces near the Barrack Field, in the occupation of Samuel Seabrook and William Axon, and owned by Mr. Philpot.
Land adjoining the Hornchurch Road in the occupation of Mr. Tolbut and belonging to Mrs. Parker.

All were deemed suitable, and the Clerk was directed to enquire from the owners as to the price they would be willing to sell two acres for.
Mr. Mashiter and Mrs. Parker decided not to sell. A Mr. Pedley offered another two acres near the Barrack Field for £525, land tax redeemed.
Mr. Philpot, who attended the Board, offered two acres at £160 an acre at the end nearest the town, or £150 an acre at the end farthest from the town, both subject to land tax redeemed. This land was next to Mr. Pedley's, and the occupier, Mr. Seabrook, was willing to give immediate possession on payment by valuation for his crops and dressings.

The Board agreed to accept Mr. Philpot's offer of the piece nearest the town, unless advised otherwise by the architect; and Messrs. Edwards, Savage and Kempthorne were invited to submit plans and estimates for a Central Workhouse for 450 paupers in six classes, and to include stabling for fifteen horses and a shed for carriages. (Parking space for the Board?).
The understanding was that the architect whose plans were accepted would be the one employed on the actual building operations, and the other two would each receive seven guineas

Buying the Land, Choosing the Builder.
Chadwell Heath's Three Windmills.
Romford and the Market; its Businesses and Shops.

57

(£7.35p) for their work in producing plans.

Three weeks later Mr. Edwards and Mr. Kempthorne presented their plans. Mr. Savage had backed out. A committee was appointed to scrutinise the plans and *'Make such alterations and improvements as they thought necessary.'*
After due consideration the committee voted the plans of Mr. Edwards be accepted by 5 votes to 4, and this was confirmed by the Board.
It then transpired that Mr. Philpot's land would be required for the projected Romford and Thameshaven Railway, (which would have connected Romford to Mucking, but which came to nothing).
However Colonel Graves, who owned land next to Mr. Philpot, offered to sell as much as might be required, also at £160 an acre, land tax redeemed. It too was occupied by farmer Seabrook for a term, three years of which were unexpired. The Building Committee decided to go and have a look at it, and to apply to the Commissioners for £9000 for the building, and £350 for the land.

In all, the Guardians agreed to purchase two and a half acres, and Mr. Seabrook was directed to dispose of the growing crop of rye for the best price he could get. Since this was the middle of May, a likely plan would have been to cut it for hay at the end of the month, but since the general belief was that good hay couldn't be made in less than five days in June, he would have had to wait until the weather was warm and settled.

The Commissioners agreed to a loan of £9000, the terms being that it would be repayable over 20 years at 4% interest. Tenders for the erection of the new Workhouse were advertised in the Chelmsford Chronicle for £2.19.6d, The Essex Standard for £1.2.6d., and in The Times and Chronicle for £2.18.0d.
As was usual at that time, the adverts. would have been placed for two consecutive weeks.

The Thameshaven Railway received its Act in 1836, for a 16 mile line from Romford to the Thames at Shell Haven. Land was purchased but there were delays in construction and only the line from Thames Haven to Mucking was opened, on 7th. June, 1855, and that having been previously purchased by The London Tilbury & Southend line in 1854.

Estimates soon arrived from the builders, including the following:-

Mr. William Sherwood, Belvedere Rd. Lambeth: £13,883.10.0
Messrs. G.& S. Sharp, Commercial Rd.   "   : £11.854.10.0
      "   Locke & Nelson, Theobalds Rd.,   : £10,887.0.0.
      "   Cove & Bartlett, Romford.   : £10,154.0.0
      "   Curtis & Son, Stratford.   : £ 9,249.0.0.
      Mr. H.S. Smith. Dockhead.   : £8,729.0.0.
Messrs. Steggles & Son, Bury St. Edmunds.   : £8,709.0.0.

this last figure to be reduced by £50 if the gravel on the site found fit for making concrete.

Price was undoubtedly the ruling factor, and subject to sureties being acceptable, the Board unanimously agreed to take the Steggles tender.

In the meantime Mr. Offin, estate agent, advised the Board that in answer to their request, he put a value of £50 on farmer Seabrook's rye crop. Seabrook didn't bother to make hay, but sold it green for £12.10.0d, and the Board made up the sum with a cheque for £37.10.0d.

At the same time Colonel and Mrs. Graves signed the deed of conveyance for the land and a cheque for £400 was passed to them.

On reading through the terms of the contract, Messrs Steggles couldn't agree to some clauses, and wrote and told the Board so. The Board in their turn, thought the terms not unusual and that they were in accordance with the original specification sent out, so they determined not to modify the contract. The following week, Mr. Steggles and Mr. Edwards the architect both attended the Board's meeting, where drawings and specifications were read over, and eventually signed by the builder.

Buying the Land, Choosing the Builder.
Chadwell Heath's Three Windmills.
Romford and the Market; its Businesses and Shops.

59

At this meeting it was agreed too, that a Clerk of Works be hired at £2.10.0d. Per week, and at a separate meeting it was agreed to pay Mr. Edwards 4% of the cost of the building, or something approaching £380.

The total sum to be raised on loan for building the new Workhouse was reckoned to be £9,450., and this sum would have to be repaid over the years. Responsibility for raising Poor Rates still of course rested with the individual parish Vestries, hence this sum would ultimately fall into their collective laps, albeit with twenty years to pay it off.

To this end the contributions due from each parish, calculated from the 'averages' mentioned in chapter 2, would range from £3,806 for Barking, down to £91 for little Wennington.

All this, in addition to the Poor Rates now running at £1,930 for the whole Union for the current Quarter, made a daunting sum. It is easy to see now why the Board of Guardians had tried so hard to manage with the existing Houses, one in Barking, one in Romford, and thus avoid this massive additional expenditure.

On 11th. September, 1838, the Chairman and vice Chairman journeyed up to London for a meeting with the Commissioners for the Loan of Exchequer Bills, and returned with the following:- 1 Bill for £1,000, 14 Bills for £500, and 7 Bills for £100. This made a total of £8,700, the builder's tender only, with nothing towards the cost of the land, payment to farmer Seabrook, or any other of the incidental expenses.

They deposited the Bills with the Treasurers, Messrs. Johnson's Bank, but directed the bank to sell the £1,000 Bill. *The produce to be placed to the credit of the Union.'* It duly changed hands for £1,004.18.4d. And the £4.18.4d. Was placed meticulously to the 'Interest Account'.

Everything was now in place for work to begin, as the parishes of the Union, and indeed the whole of England , approached

In common with the rest of the country, the population of the Union was rapidly increasing as shown by the latest quarterly returns for births and deaths:-

	Births.	Deaths.
Barking	45	27
Ilford	40	20
Romford	20	26
Dagenham	9	9
Hornchurch	14	21
Upminster	9	3
Rainham	6	2
Warley	3	1
Cranham	4	1
Wennington	0	1
	150	111

what was to be a winter of exceptional severity.

And in that blowy autumn of 1838, Romford, like Ilford, found itself as something of a staging post for the coaches to and fro en route from London to the East Anglian towns of Colchester, Ipswich, Bury St. Edmunds and Norwich. The passage of so many coaches and wagons each day automatically quickened the pace; added a note of urgency to the town.

But what gave Romford its character, its sense of importance, of individuality, was its market. Romford had long formed a partnership with the surrounding countryside; for the market needed the farmers and their produce equally as much as the farms and farmers needed it. Market days were on Tuesdays and Wednesdays – there was no Saturday market until 1907. Thomas Bird, in his hand written book 'Havering and Romford', all in beautiful copperplate, and dated 1869, recalls the market of his youth, thirty years before;-

'Stirring and important times, especially on that day of all days the most exciting and eventful - the market day, when pigs in their sties, calves in their pens, and cattle and horses in the street, filled up the whole town from the loam pond (the bottom end of the market place where the old Laurie cinema used to be) *to the White Hart. To squeeze in among the farmers in the road from the corners of Hornchurch and Collier Row lanes was a work of no little difficulty. The rich and the poor, the men and the boys, the women and the children, amid the clamour of the buyers and the sellers, the shouts of the drovers, the bellowing of bulls and calves, and the gentle bleating of sheep made up a melange of a most exciting and extraordinary character. The memories of the old market day can never be obliterated. It is somewhat different now (1869), the dirty old shambles* (situated between The Lamb and St. Edwards church, and where animals were butchered) *have been removed, the cattle are tied up, the pig and calf pens improved, and the farmers*

Buying the Land, Choosing the Builder.
Chadwell Heath's Three Windmills.
Romford and the Market, its businesses and Shops.

61

THE THREE MILLS, CHADWELL HEATH.

(From an old painting made about 1810).

[To face p. 263.

THE POND IN FRONT OF THE MILLER'S HOUSE WOULD HAVE BEEN
FOR THE HORSES DRAWING THE CORN WAGONS TO DRINK AT.

RUSTY BACON.

Buying the Land, Choosing the Builder.
Chadwell Heath's Three Windmills.
Romford and the Market; its Businesses and Shops.

63

have a market place to themselves. The free and easy style of the old has in great degree passed away, and has given place to the more stiff and orderly, although still bustling formalities of the new.'

Again, William Howitt in his book 'Rural Life of England', which he published in 1838, paints a general picture of country folk heading for the market, that could well have applied to Romford, catching as it does, the bustle and anticipation.

'There are few things that give one such a feeling of the pros-perity of the country, as seeing the country people pour into a large market town on market day. There they come, streaming along all the roads that lead to it from the wide country around. The footpaths are filled with a hardy and homely suc-cession of pedestrians, men and women, with their baskets on their arms, containing their butter, eggs, apples, mushrooms, walnuts, nuts, elderberries, bundles of herbs, young pigeons, fowls, or whatever happens to be in season. There are boys and girls too, similarly loaded, and also with baskets of birds nests in Spring, cages of young birds, baskets of tame rabbits, bunches of cowslips and primroses and all kind of flowers and country productions imaginable. The carriage road is equally alive with people riding and driving along; farmers and coun-try gentlemen, country clergy, parish overseers, and various other personages, drawn to the market town by some real or imagined business; are rattling forward on horseback, or in carriages of various kinds, gigs and spring carts, and carts without springs. There are carriers wagons and covered carts without end, many of them showing from their open fronts whole troops of women, snugly seated.'

In the case of Romford, he might have added too, the droves of cattle and sheep, and the loads of pigs, headed for market.

As for boys with baskets of birds nests, whilst today such a thing would be a sure fire recipe for prompt arrest, in early

Victorian times there was indeed a market for them. They varied in price from a penny upwards, depending on the bird, and of course they had to be filled with a clutch of eggs.

Often they were bought as a novelty, and they were also in demand by taxidermists who mounted birds in glass cases, when the nests would add authenticity to the arrangement.

Henry Mayhew, in his massive 'London Labour, London Poor' published in 1851, gives a long account of an interview with a street seller of birds nests. The young man was very knowledgeable, and tells how he would walk barefoot from London to Chelmsford and Witham to gather nests from the hedgerows; or just to Romford if the weather was bad.

He also caught and sold snakes, lizards, snails and frogs; snails by the bucketful. Farmers it seemed, didn't object to his birds-nesting, they saw it as a way of keeping down the numbers that raided their corn.

Typical of Mayhew, having listened carefully to the young man's tale of genuine misfortune that had driven him to ply this trade, he rigged him out with a suit of clothes, and gave him money to start in one of the better street trades.

Howitt however, was a member of the gentry, and his description of ordinary folk off to market was undoubtedly on the rosy side. He wanted country folk to look warm, comfortable, well fed, satisfied. After all, he wanted to preserve the status quo. Farm rents, and thus his income, were high, and as far as he and his ilk were concerned this pleasurable state of affairs could go on for ever. The Corn Laws were still in place, land-owners filled the seats in Parliament and governed still in spite of the (modest) widening of the electorate brought about by The Great Reform Act, and for his money, long may it remain so.

Sadly for him, change was under way; coming events were casting their shadows before them. The rumblings against the

---

SMALLPOX.

Mr. Edward Collier, Churchwarden of Romford, having wrongfully ordered the admission of a girl, Emma Patmore who was in his service and who was *'labouring under smallpox'* was ordered to pay 7d. To the Board, for her stay in the Workhouse.

It was ordered that no person shall in future be admitted to either Workhouse whom the M.O. has declared to be labouring under an infectious disease, but that all such applications shall if necessary be referred to the Relieving Officer.

Was she then sent, home?

Buying the Land, Choosing the Builder.
Chadwell Heath's Three Windmills.
Romford and the Market; its Businesses and Shops.

65

Corn Laws were growing ever louder; Cobden and Bright, founders of the Anti Corn Law League, were now vociferously debating in Parliament; William Cobbet, the radical, was printing pamphlets by the thousand.

If the Corn Laws were repealed, the price of corn would collapse – or so the farmers thought – and the threat of this put them under pressure, for many of them had long leases taken out at high rents, and those rents would still have to be found.

The farmer's response to all this was to buckle to and to farm more productively than ever, and this was especially true of those around Romford. One area of intensive and scientific farming was Havering, transformed by men like John Heaton of Bedfords, James Ellis of Park Farm and Collinson Hall of Bower Farm, all of whose land was described as *'In a high state of cultivation, and great crops of corn and green food for cattle have been obtained.'*

James Ellis, by the way, grew hops on his farm, and also over in Kent, and was said to be the largest grower of hops in the world! Could there be a connection between this and that entry in the Romford Workhouse Labour Book concerning 'Hops sold for the quarter: £3.8.3d., and Romford labour: 13/3d, mentioned in chapter 4? Were indeed the paupers sent out to Havering Park Farm to pick hops?

And what was meant by 'intensive and scientific farming'? It would certainly have included land drainage by the use of stones or the newly available hollow drain tiles, laid at the bot tom of trenches dug herringbone fashion below the ploughing depth, across hitherto boggy fields. It meant also liming, and fertilising the land with guano and that newly available by - product of the steel industry, superphosphate. It would also have entailed drilling in seed instead of broadcasting it by hand, thus enabling horse drawn hoeing between the rows of corn. It meant adopting crop rotation, like the popular Norfolk

The collection of Poor Rates both for Outdoor Relief and for running the Workhouses was on a scale now, that required the employment of full time Rate Collectors. Two were needed and they were paid at a poundage of 8d. in the £ for rates less than £3, and 4d. in the £ for rates greater than £3.
Thus Collector Beadle:

Sums under £3	Poundage
£393.16.8d	£13.2.6d
Sums over £3	
£522.12.2d	£8.14.2d

Four Course, of wheat followed by turnips, which allowed hoeing and thus cleaning the land of weeds, then oats or barley, and finally clover, which last enriched the soil ready for wheat again.

It meant too, keeping abreast of technical innovations like the newly introduced threshing machines, and also the grazing and rearing of the much improved breeds of cattle and sheep now available. In this way a farmer could improve the productivity of his acres by several fold.

In Romford on market day there was undoubtedly an air of prosperity, but it wasn't shared by the farmworker and his family. His wage had gone up very little if at all; it was cheaper to eat potatoes than bread, and meat was no everyday commodity. There was an increasing polarisation of society; the rich were getting richer, the poor were standing still. Romford, and the Board of Guardians were about to build a Workhouse for 450 paupers. 450 out of a total population of 20,500 is only 2%, but the truth was that at least another 10% were in dire need.

Not that Romford was about to throw its hands in the air in despair. Opportunity, it seemed abounded everywhere. Edward Ind, who had bought The Star public house together with its little brewery back in 1799, was watching his business steadily grow. In partnership now, with a Mr. Smith, he was tendering successfully against Woodfines, the Hornchurch brewer, for the supply of beer to the Workhouse:-

1838. Beer for the 1st. Quarter: Woodfines   £1.13.0d a barrel
       "   "   " 2nd   "   : Ind & Smith £1.12.0d " "
       "   "   " 3rd   "   : Woodfines   £1.11.0d " "

And so it went on. Tenacity was the name of the game, and by 1842 Ind & Smith had won the day with a price of £1.3.0d a barrel. It was not until 1845 that the brewery succeeded to its

Buying the Land, Choosing the Builder.
Chadwell Heath's Three Windmills.
Romford and the Market; its Businesses and Shops.

67

latter day name, when the brothers Octavius and George Coope replaced Mr. Smith in the partnership.

The Hornchurch brewery, Woodfines, was situated opposite The Kings Head as you start to go up the hill towards St. Andrews church. John Woodfine had set up the brewery ten years before Edward Ind in 1789. It remained in the family until 1874, failed in 1889, was built up again business-wise and finally sold to Mann Crossman and Paulin in 1925. It had forty public houses at that time, and having acquired the outlets, they promptly closed the brewery down.

Although Romford couldn't boast a major employer, there were, in addition to the many shops and suppliers, numerous small but doubtless thriving enterprises. These included several workshops in metalworking and engineering, like Martins in the High Street and Underwoods in Lamb Yard, and Randalls in Collier Row. There was too a coachbuilder called Slipper in the High Street. Slipper's business was ultimately taken over by Messrs. Allen Bros., which survived until 1975 as the motor engineers.
Macarthy's, the chemist – he with the seat on the Board of Guardians – also had a mineral water factory in the Market Place. Among the shops in the town, Pigot's Directory for 1839 lists 10 bakers, 12 butchers, 2 cheesemongers, 4 coal merchants 7 grocers and tea dealers, 9 fishmongers and fruiterers (?), 2 farriers, 18 public houses, 9 tailors, and 6 straw hat makers - 5 of them women.

Running ahead a little, a Corn Exchange was opened in1845 in a converted building adjoining the Golden Lion. Johnsons Baank we have already mentioned. There was too, a branch of The London and County Bank, and also The Romford Savings Bank, with branches in Brentwood, Billericay, Orsett and Ongar. By the year 1846, this bank had deposits of no less than £71,802 belonging to 2421 depositors, several

There was even a fire engine, horse-drawn of course and with hand pumps. An engine house was built for it in the garden of the old Workhouse, and this was retained when in 1840 the latter was sold off.

charitable societies, and 7 Friendly Societies.

Like Barking and Ilford, Romford also had its gasworks, established in 1825 by George Bell and situated in South Street (then called Hornchurch lane), opposite Eastern Road. Like the others, its product was used in the first instance mainly to light the town centre. In 1847 it became The Romford Gas and Coke Co.

Building was going on apace. 200 Artisans cottages and two factories were built on the eight acres of the old Barrack Field. One of the factories opened as Spencer's Comb Works, and the district became known as New Romford.

The Barrack Field covered the area now enclosed by Waterloo Road, St. Andrews Road, and Queen Street, and originally had six troops of Cavalry quartered there during the Napoleonic Wars. The Barracks buildings had been demolished in 1825.

Long before Rowland Hill introduced Penny Post in 1840 with its prepaid one penny adhesive stamps, there was a well established postal network in the area; Barking and Ilford indeed had a local penny post district going back to the 1790's. The Romford Post Office was in the Market Place and was by all accounts very busy. Letters by 2d. Post from London arrived daily at 11.30 am. And 6.00 pm., and were despatched in the opposite direction at 9.00 am. And 4.00 pm. There was also a service to Ongar, Horndon-on-the-Hill, Grays, and Dagenham.

Things were beginning to move on the civic front too. In 1819 the Romford Lighting and Paving Act set up a body of Commissioners with power to levy rates not exceeding two shillings in the pound, for paving, lighting, watching and cleansing.

The Commission consisted of the vicar, all the resident magistrates, the surveyors of highways (as appointed by the Vestry), and twenty-four others, all appointed not elected yet, like the Guardians. In spite of the size of this body, their remit was

Buying the Land, Choosing the Builder.
Chadwell Heath's Three Windmills.
Romford and the Market; its Businesses and Shops.

69

quite restricted, applying only to the area of the Market Place, High Street, and adjoining areas of North Street and South Street.

This district, as we have seen, soon got gas lighting. The amount of light produced by the lamps was nothing special, the gas simply burned as a luminous flame via a fishtail burner.

Paving meant the pedestrian pavements; the carriageways, the main ones of which although kept in good order, still had only gravel surfaces (asphalt was still some years away).

Turning to children's education in Romford at this time; as in Barking and Ilford, there was a sprinkling of Dame's schools and the like, but the foremost establishment was St. Edward's Church of England primary school. It united with the National Society's school, and in 1835 a new schoolroom was opened. In that year 165 boys and 90 girls were being taught by a master and a mistress and the use of monitors. Monitors were akin to apprentice teachers; often drawn from the brightest pupils in the class, they worked under the guidance of the teachers proper. The National School children wore distinguishing badges, and paid one penny per week.

Very much in keeping with the time, it is good to find that a Literary and Mechanics Institute for men had been opened in Romford in 1848.

Incandescent gas mantles didn't come in until the introduction of Electric lighting created its own strong competition.

RUMFORD, ESSEX.

THIS DRAWING BY C.B. CAMPION, AND PUBLISHED IN 1831, WITH THE SHAMBLES IN
FRONT OF THE CHURCH, MUST ACCORD CLOSELY WITH THE WAY THOMAS BIRD
REMEMBERED THE MARKET PLACE WHEN HE PUT PEN TO PAPER IN HIS DESCRIPTIVE
AND LIVELY 'HAVERING AND ROMFORD'.

7. BUILDING THE NEW WORK – HOUSE.

In the middle of September, 1838 the task of erecting the new central Union Workhouse commenced, and Messrs. Steggles the builders, no doubt anxious to make progress before the winter weather set in with its inevitable hold-ups, had set about laying the foundations right away.

Payment was to be by stages according to the amount of work completed, and within a fortnight the architect was able to report that the first stage had been accomplished *'In a good and workmanlike manner.'* to the value of £870.

The terms of the contract decreed that payment to the value of two-thirds only, of the work done, was to be made at each stage so a cheque for £580 was handed over accordingly.

It is clear that approval and payment for the work was to be in ten stages, £870 being on tenth of the £8709 tender that won Messrs. Steggles the job.

Just three weeks later a second instalment of £580 was paid, and to raise the necessary cash the Board sold two of its £500 Exchequer Bills, which in the event fetched £1008.18.4d

The original terms of the loan to cover the building costs had been that it should be repayable over twenty years at 4% interest. However, this arrangement must have gone out of the window along with the original promise to lend £9,000 at the time when the Exchequer Bills were actually handed to the Board Chairman. As we have seen, the loan had been trimmed to £8,700 only, and judging by a letter now sent by the Guardians to the Lords of the Treasury, the terms now stood at repayment over ten years only, and at 5% interest. The Board's letter sought to re-establish the original terms.

The Clerk of Works no doubt had a temporary office on the site, and taking account of the wintry weather, the entry in the Minutes for 5th. February, 1839 Reads:-
Clerk of Works 13 weeks salary £32.10.0, plus 12/-d for 15 bushels of coke for his office and 2/9d. for stationery and post.

Day to day supervision of the building work was in the hands of the Clerk of the Works, a man called Medway, who was to receive a salary of £32.10.0d a quarter.
Eight weeks after work commenced, a third instalment of £580 was paid out, this time with an additional £6 awarded as a gratuity to the workmen *'For their good conduct in the completion of the walls and roof.'* The new building, already insured for £3,000, had its cover with The Royal Exchange Assurance office extended by a further £2,000, the new premium payable now being £15.13.6d. per annum.

Mr. Pearce, the Chairman of the Board, together with Assistant Commissioner Wade and the Board's Clerk, Mr. Griffin went and looked over the work in progress. Mr. Wade suggested that the Board might think about buying the remainder of the field on which it stood. Work continued to proceed smoothly, and by the third week in January of the new year a fourth and fifth instalment had been paid to Messrs. Steggles.

The Christmas season had come and gone, and the Board's accounts, so crammed with every kind of transaction, showed once again absolutely no allowance or expenditure for the celebration of this festival, to lift the gloom for a day for the inmates of either the Barking or the Romford House. No mention either of any outside benevolence being bestowed upon them this year.

By early March, the question of the Workhouse drainage had been settled. The Board authorised Mr. Edwards to *'Construct a drain for 700 feet under the footpath and then to be carried across the road into the ditch on the south side.'* Mr. Philpot, the owner of the adjoining land having given his permission.
Then possibly the weather interrupted the work, for when the builders applied for a sixth instalment, it was withheld; the architect not feeling justified in granting it.

'There is not sufficient work finished, although the materials are on the spot.' However, a fortnight later he certified that £600 worth of work had been completed since the last instalment, and a payment of £400 was made. Another fortnight and a further payment of £180 brought the figure up to the £580 for the sixth tranche.

Meanwhile, the affairs of the Union continued to be attended to in routine fashion. At the beginning of April the annual elections for members of the Board took place. Most were returned unopposed, only those representing Romford being contested.

The Romford House, like the other properties in the town centre, was liable for Watching, Paving and 'Lamp' rates, and two demands, for 22nd. March, and 25th September last, were paid up with a cheque for £3.4.0d. – the Board could obviously be very lax in paying outstanding bills.

Estimates for the total Poor Relief for the coming Quarter were found to be £1,890, ranging from £800 for Barking down to just £10 for Wennington.

A constant stream of instructions emanated from Somerset House, including one dated 3rd. April prohibiting (again) Outdoor Relief to able-bodied paupers except in cases of sudden and urgent necessity, or sickness; with bills to be posted by Relieving Officers in their respective districts notifying this.

Parishes were being pressed to produce new tithe maps and valuation books. The supervision of this was yet another task to be taken on by the Guardians, who advertised in the usual newspapers for tenders for preparing these for Romford.

Someone pointed out that a map of the whole Liberty of Havering made *'At the time of the Inclosure* (1836) *and very accurate,'* might be made available for the new survey and valuation of Romford. A letter was written to a Mr. Walter enquiring the cost of copying that part comprising Romford,

In the midst of all this, the Board still found time to deal with little, humbler matters:-

There was the case of Sarah Loot, 12 years and the eldest of six children, her mother soon to be confined again. The Board, after due deliberation, allowed her ten shillings *'For clothes to enable her to keep a situation with Mr. Edwards at Mr. Reynolds farm near Ilford; the Clerk to write to the Commissioners explaining why the Guardians had departed from their strict rule in this instance.'*

including any recent alterations in the enclosures, plus a book of the reformed valuations *'As prescribed by the Poor Law Commissioners.'*

Mr. Walter submitted his estimate, either to copy the map on its present scale, or on a scale of 3 chains to the inch (1 chain = 22 yards). In sight of this, the Board looked again at the tenders received in response to their newspaper adverts. There were no fewer than 21 of these for the map making, and 13 for making the valuations – fair profits to be made out of this work then!

Both the survey map and the valuation went to W. Roberts, of 68, Chancery Lane; the map to be 3 chains to the inch, with 1 chain to the inch for the town, work to commence on 1st. September, and to be completed within six months. The maps to be copyright reserved until after the Commutation is completed under a penalty of £150., the Board to be at liberty to order any number of copies, with not more than 3 at 2d. an acre per copy including the valuation books. (Fields and buildings were simply numbered on the tithe maps, and the valuations were entered in the books against these numbers).

Payment for the work to be in two months after the approval by the Commissioners. Mr. Roberts to attend appeals (against the valuations) for up to two years after the initial Rate was made, on receiving five days notice, and being paid three guineas a day if the Rate confirmed, and one guinea only if the Rate quashed or amended

This last would act as an incentive to get it right first time, and all of this is an indication of how hotly contested and how much of an irritation tithes had become over the years.

Back at the building site a committee of Guardians was formed to supervise completion and fitting out of the new House. *'They to report their proceedings from time to time to the Board.'*

A seventh instalment of £850 was paid to the builders, but then in May Mr. Edwards reported that *'The works going on were not being pushed as rapidly as they ought to be.'* Steggles were instructed *'to proceed with more activity.'*

From this point on, problems over the payment to Messrs. Steggles began to creep in. There followed a stream of litigation and demands for payment from banks and others representing Steggles, not without acrimony at times. It is the writer's conclusion that the great bulk of the work had been completed, but that either Steggles had gone broke, or old Mr. Steggles had died leaving some confusion pending his Will going through probate.

It soon became clear that getting money out of our Board was like drawing teeth. If, on the one hand a fool and his money are soon parted, then on the other, the Board's attitude throughout was such that 'Financial Caution' properly belonged as their middle name.

However, at the end of September, the 8th. And 9th. instalments were paid out, with a further £1000 in November, but leaving the matter still not completely cleared up. This saga was by no means ended yet, but in the meantime the shell of the New Union Workhouse had finally been completed, and the Clerk of the Works was paid off with the appraisal *'That the Board fully appreciated the attention, talent, and integrity with which he had discharged his duties.'*

Great strides were now being made in fitting out the House, deciding on staffing, and so on. Mr. And Mrs. Sellars, the Master and Matron at Barking, were to be appointed to the New House. Quite naturally, they asked for a raise in salary; it was after all, a much bigger Workhouse; but no luck, at least for a start their wages were to remain the same as before, at £60.10.0 for him, and £50.10.0d for her.

The Master at Romford was given his notice, to take effect when the old House closed down; and for Mrs. Taylor, the

In January '39, Mr. Miller, Master at Romford, applied for the post of Master of Epsom Workhouse. The Board's Reference for him read:-
'Duly appreciating the very accurate manner in which Mr. Miller has kept his accounts and his extremely correct conduct as Master of the Romford Workhouse and believing him to be fully capable of managing a Workhouse in a rural district, have much pleasure in expressing the favourable opinion they entertain of him.'

However, Mr. Miller must have been unlucky, for on 25th. June, the Clerk was asked to write to the Commissioners for permission to award him a gratuity of £25 *'In consideration of his assuidity and attention to the duties of his office.'*

Romford Matron, arrangements were made for her to reside in the New House, with double rations, which is to say, to eat at the Master's table. This all probably indicated that she was of retiring age.

In the matter of water, there was of course no mains supply anywhere in the Union; needs were met by way of wells and pumps. Water, and lots of it would be required for an establishment with an expected five hundred or so inmates, so tenders were put out for sinking a well. The successful applicant was a Mr. Bartlett, who undertook to do the job at the following cost:-

For a depth of 33 feet:	£125.0.0d
Deduct for every foot less:	£3.5.0d
Add for every foot more:	£4.5.0d
Up to seven foot deeper.	

Six weeks later a sample of the well water was brought to a meeting of the Board for them to taste. It didn't altogether meet with approval, so the architect was instructed to have Mr. Bartlett pump the well out twice, the quality of the water then to be tried again, and if approved of, *'The bottoms of the cesspools of the privies be raised a little, as well as the sides rendered in cement in order to prevent any drainage from them to the well.'* The well and its water must have eventually been deemed satisfactory, for Mr. Batrlett was given an interim payment at the end of August of £80, with a final cheque the following December for £48.13.6d., making this total bill £128.13.6d., very close to his original estimate.

Obviously, as much as possible that could be re-used was to be transferred from the old Houses to the New Union Workhouse, but the changeover also gave an opportunity to renew old worn out items.

Beds were among such articles, and two tenders were obtained

for their supply. That of Mr. Wedlake, the Hornchurch
ironfounder, was accepted, his prices being:-

Mens beds	6ft. x 4ft. 2ins.	£1.6.6d.
" "	6ft. x 2ft. 6ins.	19/6d.
Girls double beds	5ft. x 3ft. 1ins.	19/6d.
" single "	5ft. x 2ft. 4ins.	16/6d.

The above to include painting twice, and old beds to be bought
back at 4/6d. Per foot for cast iron, 5/- per foot wrought iron.
One hundred beds were ordered.

More sackings and appointments – rationalising and down-
sizing. We may think that these are modern tools of management; far from it, our men on the Board were well up in all
that.

Mr. William Jones, the porter at Romford, and Mr. Wilding,
the schoolmaster at Barking were informed that their services
would not be required after Michaelmas next.

Alexander Marshall of Romford was appointed schoolmaster,
with a salary of £20 per annum plus board and lodging. In addition to his other duties he was to act as clerk to the chapel.
Miss Pepper was appointed schoolmistress at a similar salary,
and also with board and lodging.

Mr. Edwards' report on the fittings required for the kitchen
laundry and offices having been approved, estimates were prepared and tenders were put out for the necessary work to be
done by stovemakers and ironmongers. Those who submitted
tenders were called in and the architect explained further detail
of what was required. As ever, the job was awarded to the lowest tender, submitted by a Mr. Steadman at £138, with James
White, fruiterer of the Mile End Road named as his surety.

Mr. Steadman, who had some experience in this line of
work, suggested that instead of a number of separate fires, the
whole might be supplied from one boiler, and he invited the
Board to view the installation put up by him at Bethnall Green

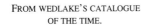

FROM WEDLAKE'S CATALOGUE
OF THE TIME.

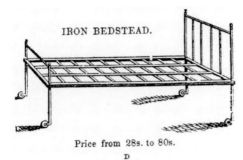

IRON BEDSTEAD.

Price from 28s. to 80s.

D

Workhouse. He subsequently prepared a set of plans for steam apparatus with a high pressure boiler which would deliver steam to the two wash houses and to the female probationary wards also, at an extra cost of £148.

The Board determined to evaluate the saving in coal that this would bring, and asked the Masters at Romford and Barking to take accurate account of the fuel consumed in one week for washing and cooking. Their conclusion was that the installation of such a boiler would save them no more than £20 a year, so they decided to stick to the original plans, which Mr. Steadman proceeded with. However, when the final account was paid, the sum total came to £241.10.4d., much closer to the estimate for the steam boiler. Perhaps they were persuaded to install it after all.

At this time tenders for slate baths and washing trays (?for the laundry) were opened and the contract, worth £63.10.0d., was given to Messrs. Cooper & Son.

A Porter was appointed, name of Francis Hobbs. His wage was to be £15 a year and full board, together with a coat and hat to the value of £5.

The post of Chaplain was advertised; his duties to include to preach twice on Sundays, attend the Workhouse every day to read prayers, to visit the sick, and to superintend the moral and religious education of the children.

It was resolved that Mr. Butter and Mr. Bowers be appointed Medical Officers to the New House, they to attend alternately for a quarter, Mr. Butter to take the first quarter, terminating at Lady Day next. Their salaries were fixed at £15 a quarter, for which they should attend daily.

Out of a considerable number of applicants, the Rev. Edwards was appointed chaplain on the 10th. December, 1839. Three weeks later, on the last day of the old year, the Board received a letter stating that the chaplain *'Had been in a state of disgraceful intoxication on the 24th. Instant.'* Also a letter from the Bishop of London stating that in consequence of information received he had suspended Edwards and prohibited him from officiating until he had cleared himself of the charge.

The rev. Edwards was staying at the house of Noah Dunnet, Guardian, who also produced a written statement of the facts. Edwards was interviewed by the Chairman and another member, the rev. Dr. Robinson, who stated that they were satisfied that the charge had been exaggerated; that they would communicate their findings to the Bishop, and if he, the Bishop saw no objections, he should be allowed to return to his duties.
Alas, things did not go well for this poor man who had partaken inadvertently of too much Christmas cheer, for following a conversation between the Chairman and the Bishop, the rev. Edwards tendered his resignation, and was paid a cheque for £10 for his services.

Back to the water situation. An adequate pump was needed, and a man was sent to examine the one at Poplar (old) Workhouse, and to report on its condition and value. This drew a blank, so the task of assembling a pumping engine was awarded to a Mr. Robert Morton, subject to the work being approved either by Mr. Edwards or an engineer, and to cost £78.10.0d., the work to be completed by 22nd. November.
To protect it from the weather, and also to protect the paupers who would man the pump, a shed was erected over it, together with an adjoining scullery, at a cost of £69 in what was to be the boy's yard.

Improvements, and a table for the Boardroom were taken in hand. Messrs. Bartlett & Sons, - carpenters and general builders in addition to well diggers - undertook to make the table and also a bookcase for £38.5.0d, and to carry out various other jobs.

Everything had to be provided for. An eight day clock with

This Bartlett contract throws light on the daily rate earned by tradesmen at this time:-

Stonemason:	6/-d	per day.
Bricklayer:	4/4d	" "
Plasterer:	5/-d	" "
Labourer:	2/8d	" "

Stock bricks were £2.5.0d per 1000
Lime   13/6d for 18 bushels.

two dials was to be put up, price £9., and indeed, time itself was running on.

The mill situated in the Romford House was to be transferred, and Mr. Carter, the millwright was directed to fix it in the New House *'As soon as possible, and to make such alterations as necessary for working the mill from the vagrant ward as well as the able-bodied ward.'*

A new mangle was ordered, the old one to be sold.

It was December again, just a fortnight before Christmas. The Board had held its first weekly meeting in the New House two months earlier. At last, all seemed to be ready.

What we today have come to call The Oldchurch Workhouse, crouched, forgotten in a corner of the Hospital grounds; stood then, splendid, isolated from the town. Its yellow stock bricks and shining slate roof unsullied yet by smoke and grime, caught perhaps in a shaft of winter sunlight, it made a striking and forbidding sight of dread and disgrace to any man standing on the abyss of penury and despair.

To the Board of Guardians it represented something of a triumph.

8. ALL THE UNION'S VILLAGES.

Despite the ever quickening pace of activity at the new Union Workhouse, out in the broad acres of the parishes life moved on at its even tenor, punctuated from time to time by those events which signalled the gathering changes of the century's progress.

Barking, like Romford, had been prevailed upon to produce a new survey map for the tithings, and the contract for its drawing had been signed. The town had asked to be allowed to let out their Workhouse once its inmates had been transferred to Romford. To that end a Mr. Harvey had already been asked to auction off any fixtures and things left behind in the empty building.

The Churchwardens, Overseers and inhabitants of Romford had made a similar request, but in their case they wished to sell the House and grounds once it was vacated. The Commissioners replied to Romford directing them to convene a meeting within twenty one days to discuss the matter. This they did, but requested more time than the thirty days suggested by the Commissioners, in which to make the sale.

Hornchurch, in the 1830's and 40's was a large industrial village. Its architecture had changed little over the years; as late as 1917 it was described as 'generally of the 17th. Century', and included a number of large houses such as Fairkytes, the home of Thomas Wedlake the ironfounder, and later Joseph Fry, the son of Elizabeth Fry the prison reformer. John Bearblock, vice chairman of the Board of Guardians, lived at Hornchurch Hall, which could indeed trace its roots back to the 17th. Century and beyond; but Langtons, the largest private residence in the village, was Georgian in architecture.

The parish was large, 6783 acres, with many sizeable mixed farms. Enclosure of farmland had long been the order of the day. More recently, following an act of 1811, Redden Court Green, Ardleigh Green, and Squirrels Heath were all enclosed, no doubt to the detriment of the local inhabitants.

The leather industry, for which the village had been famous in medieval times when the High Street was known as Pell (Pelt) Street, had all but disappeared, but Messrs. Bright and Beardwell kept the last tannery open until 1846, and James Fry of North Street remained in business as a fellmonger right up to 1870.

Of the 2186 population, most were employed on the farms, but there was also Woodfine's Brewery, already mentioned, and the brick and tile works which lay back behind the High Street, just before Abbs Cross Lane, or South End Road as it was then called. This latter was owned by Charles Cove who became an active member of the Board of Guardians.

The chief industry of the village was the ironfoundry in Billet Lane belonging to Thomas and Robert Wedlake. This they had established in 1810, with a second foundry, the Union Foundry, opened in the High Street in 1846. Wedlakes were busy, employing some eighty or ninety hands at a dozen forges. They had the ear of the farming community, and had designed and built a variety of farm implements, several of which earned awards at the increasingly popular County Agricultural Shows. After the death of Thomas, the business carried on under the name of Mary, his wife.

Hornchurch had its complement of shops and trades, and there was the windmill at the back of the Dell, beside the church. Like Romford, Hornchurch too had invested in a fire engine; acquired in 1830, it had cost £18.10.0d

There were nine inns in the parish, those in the village included

THE FRONT COVER OF WEDLAKE'S
CATALOGUE

———

By Her Majesty's Royal Letters Patent.

HONOURED WITH SEVERAL MEDALS FROM THE ROYAL SOCIETY
OF AGRICULTURE:

MODERN AND IMPROVED

Agricultural Implement Manufactory,

Established in Essex upwards of Forty Years.

MARY WEDLAKE & COMPY

OF THE

FAIRKYTES IRON-WORKS, NEAR ROMFORD,

(LONDON HOUSE,)

118, FENCHURCH STREET, CITY,

AND AT 8, BILLITER STREET,

AND STAND No. 5, NEW CORN EXCHANGE, MARK LANE.

———

TO AGRICULTURISTS, COLONISTS, EMIGRANTS, ETC.

MARY WEDLAKE (Widow) AND COMPANY, of the Original Iron-Works and Agricultural Implement Manufactory, (Established upwards of Forty years,) at 118, FENCHURCH STREET, (Opposite MARK LANE,) London, beg to inform their Friends they continue to manufacture all kinds of Modern Agricultural Implements, made on scientific principles, and approved of by the first farmers in England.

Being assisted by men of talent in the Manufacture of these Articles, MARY WEDLAKE & COMPANY hope to deserve the high repute this Establishment has so long enjoyed, and now respectfully solicit a continuance of the patronage of the numerous friends of its late founder, Mr. THOMAS WEDLAKE.

All Letters to be addressed to MARY WEDLAKE AND COMPANY at their Counting-House, 118, Fenchurch Street, London, will be punctually attended to.

The Kings Head, The Bull (now the Fatling and Firkin), and The White Hart (Newt and Cumber). Others further out were The Cherry Tree, The Crown, at Roneo Corner, and The Albion at Dovers Corner.

A Receiving House for Post was established in 1838, but at that time there was still only one coach a day to London. No matter, Romford, with all its connections was only a couple of miles away along Hornchurch Lane as it was then known.

Once a year, on Whit. Monday, there was a pleasure fair, a pretty raucous event; but what gave Hornchurch its notoriety was its sporting connections. Every year, on Christmas Day, a wrestling match was arranged in the Dell, with the winner awarded a Boar's Head, cooked and dressed. Great crowds attended; many side bets were placed; and the winner and his cronies carried off the prize to feast on it in The Kings Head.

Even more important was the cricket. The parish had gained and sustained an enviable reputation in the game by 1830, with at that time an unbeaten record going back for seven years. Hornchurch challenged and beat an all Essex eleven in 1830, and in the following year took on no less than the MCC. At Lords, where the match was drawn, the scores for the two innings being MCC. 71 and 58, and Hornchurch 61 and 7 for no wicket. Sadly, they were comprehensively beaten on the return match, played on their own ground at Langtons before a crowd of 3,000. Unbowed, they played on for many years, beating the West Essex side in 1834. This match, played at Navestockside, included three members of the Bearblock family, one playing for Hornchurch, and John, the vice Chairman of the Board of Guardians and another (?brother) playing in the West Essex team.

HORNCHURCH. CORNER OF HIGH STREET
AND NORTH STREET.

THE BELL INN,
UPMINSTER.

CRANHAM CHURCH AND THE
VILLAGE SCHOOL.

Upminster, and its neighbour Cranham, were purely agricultural parishes in the first half of the nineteenth century.

Cranham, thinly populated with just three hundred souls, could boast very little by way of amenities, but in the spirit of the times, it tried.

It had, as we have seen, a Workhouse until 1836, housing up to a dozen inmates, and the Vestry had a contract with a local doctor to attend the poor, which dated back to 1811.

By 1839 sixteen children were being taught bible reading, writing, and needlework at a school in a cottage. Thomas Boyd, and the rector, the reverend Thomas Ludby paid for children who couldn't afford school pence. There was also an evening school at Cranham Hall; good conduct there was rewarded with gifts of clothing.

Upminster covered an area of 3,369 acres, and according to the 1831 census, out of 202 families in the parish, 134 were in agriculture. There were two windmills; one, a post mill, was on Gaynes Common, the other, the smock mill which is such a feature of present day Upminster, boasted an ancillary steam mill installed in 1818.

Like Hornchurch, there were brick kilns, situated at the junction of Hall and Bird lanes, and producing bricks, tiles and the new hollow clay drainpipes used for field drainage. What little shops and trades there were would have been clustered round the crossroads by the Bell Inn.

Upminster was also a favoured residence for successful City gentlemen and to that end a number of large estate houses in spacious grounds had been erected by the beginning of the century.

Schoolwise, Upminster seemed better endowed than Hornchurch, which until 1844, when the little National School was built next to the Chaplaincy, only boasted Ayletts school, held in the vestry for ten poor boys to learn the three R's.

THE BRICK KILN

By contrast, in Upminster in addition to a school for twenty
boys and girls and another in North Upminster with a Mistress
teaching spelling, reading and sewing; had five private schools
including John Saunders school with 37 boys, both day and
boarding.

Great Warley, the northernmost parish in the Union, was
again entirely agricultural. It was more populous than Cranham, with 424 inhabitants at the time of the '31 census.
Its links with Romford must have felt tenuous. It stood only a
mile or two from Brentwood, and in matters relating to the
Workhouse, as we have seen, before being corralled into the
Romford Union it had joined forces with the parishes in the
Ongar Hundred; although that manoeuvre could hardly have
been made on geographical grounds either. The Essex Regiment Barracks it should be said, was over the boarder in Little
Warley.

Great Warley must always
have been something of a scattered village, with The Thatchers
Arms inn at one end and The
Magpie, later called The Headley
Arms at the other end. Roads and
their upkeep may well have been
a problem judging by the re-
minder of 1843 that 'No one rated
at less than £500 might offer less
than three days duty of statute labour for the upkeep of the roads
per year.'
The running of the village in the
first half of the 19th. Century was
archetypically rural, the Vestry
being composed of the Rector or

GREAT WARLEY.

the Curate in the chair, plus 3 or 4 only, substantial farmers who took the parish offices between them.   No room for any interlopers there then.

Further evidence of the scattered nature of the parish lies in the fact that in 1833 there were not one, but three small day schools, with between them 54 pupils. Ten years later a new school was built for 70 children supported by grants from the Church of England National Society.

Havering -atte-Bower's 332 souls were dispersed about the village in cottages on the estates, rather than beside the church, or clustered round the green with its stocks and whipping post –those instruments of punishment, which although not any more used were to endure until 1976.

Situated on high ground some 350 feet above sea level, it was, as already mentioned , an area of intensive farming. The total land under cultivation amounted to some 3,200 acres, with a further 2,700 acres of pasture and 113 acres of orchard.

There were plenty of large farms – 34 over 50 acres and 9 over 200 acres. The largest of them all was Bower Farm, 1339 acres, where Collinson Hall pioneered steam ploughing in the area. He was also the first local farmer to produce milk for delivery to the London market. (At this time most of the city's milk was got from herds of cattle permanently tethered in insanitary town sheds.)

The man who farmed the tithe free Havering Park farm was James Ellis; he was the man who was reputed to be the world's largest hop grower.

The little cottage Poor House we have come across; and also the church, originally St. Mary's before it was rebuilt in the 1870's and re-consecrated St. John the Evangelist.

There were two inns; The Orange Tree and The Royal Oak.

For the children, education was in the beginning provided by Dame Tipping's school which was close by the church.

This eventually fell into ruin and was replaced in 1837 by a National Society school with places for 60 pupils supported by subscription and school pence, but 20 charity children were clothed and provided with books by Michael Field, of Pyrgo Park.

Of the three riverside parishes, Dagenham was the largest, measuring eight miles from north to south. The village centred on the church and the houses in Crown Street and at the junction with the road to Rainham. The Cross Keys inn was well established, dating as it does from the fifteenth century. Like its neighbours, market gardening was the main source of work and income for the 2,494 population. The area was famous for its produce of potatoes, peas, beans and coleseed (an old name for rape, which was grown as a green fodder crop for feeding cattle and sheep.) In addition there were almost a thousand acres of pasture adjoining the beef grazings of Barking's Rippleside.

There were six windmills including the three at Chadwell Heath, which was strictly part of Dagenham. Even as late as 1851 there were five tanners in the parish, but the main industry was always market gardening, and this was the subject of a long running dispute with the church authorities as to whether the produce should be charged at the rate of small or great tithes. No prizes for guessing which

DAGENHAM HIGH STREET.

ANGLING TICKETS FOR DAGENHAM LAKE

rate the farmers thought the more appropriate, especially when one learns that in 1844 under the Commutation Act, the great tithes alone, payable to the church of St. Peter and St. Paul were commuted to £1036 a year – well above the average tithes for the Union.

Dagenham Breach, which before it was closed off had been the cause of considerable silting up of the Thames as a result of the scouring action of the tides, was now, in the 1830's, referred to as Dagenham Lake. This was the body of water left permanently behind the new river embankment.

It belonged to a Mr. Charles Hulse, who had developed it into something of a resort for the gentry, complete with fishing; and it was at this time leased by Joseph and Elizabeth Fry, whose home was at Fairkytes in Hornchurch. They spent their summer holidays there.

The same Charles Hulse leased more, adjacent land in partnership with Edward Sage and John Burge, and together they worked a tramway, a wharf and an ice house, from which they supplied ice to Mr. Samuel Hewett for his Barking fishing fleet.

Dagenham shared with Barking a great area of Hainault forest, with over a thousand acres in the north of the parish. In 1851 an Act was passed by Parliament for the complete dis-aforestation of Hainault. In their haste and greed to release all this land for farming and market gardening, the work of cutting down the trees began soon afterwards, proceeding it was said, both night and day.

Just before the work began, claims for loss of grazing rights in the forest were heard in tawdry recognition of commoners rights. These included one submitted by William Boulton of Whalebone farm, for 20 to 30 head of cattle, 6 to 10 horses, and some swine. I wonder how cheaply he was bought off?

Next along the river bank lies Rainham, then Wennington.

With easy off-loading for 'night soil', these two parishes, like Dagenham, were producing market garden crops for London, and grazing cattle and sheep on the low lying grassy pastures of the marshes.

Rainham specialised in asparagus and was also famous for early cabbages - 'Rainham' cabbage. Almost the whole of Wennington's thirteen hundred acres lies below the twenty five foot above mean sea level mark. Peas were grown aplenty, and in the season the population of 130 or so was more than doubled by the appearance of Irish immigrant pea-pickers. The damp and the mists associated with the low lying nature of the land had earned both parishes a bad name healthwise in the past, which they found hard to dispel.

For all their seeming isolation, they were not so cut off as say Cranham or Great Warley. The landlord of Wennington's Lennard Arms inn ran a daily coach service from Horndon to London via Wennington, and a coach also ran from The Phoenix, Rainham, up to Whitechapel. There were too, the daily wagons and vans carrying produce.

The Lennard Arms had another claim to fame. Up until the early years of the century Wennington Vestry held an annual feast at this inn, usually in April. Everything, including good joints of meat, food and wine, with porter for the poor, was charged to the parish rates. It must have done a great deal for community spirit, but eventually it died out; the latest accounts I have been able to find are dated 1816, but I expect the memory lived on for many a year.

THE EXTRACT OPPOSITE, FROM THE CHELMSFORD CHRONICLE 17TH. JULY 1835, PAINTS A COLOURFUL PICTURE OF A SURPRISING DAY AT THE RACES AT WENNINGTON, NO DOUBT ENJOYED BY ALL, THE HUMBLE AS WELL AS THE RICH.

WENNINGTON RACES

The scene of animation and gaiety displayed at the social little village of Wennington far surpassed all that was ever witnessed in that retired part of the county of Essex. For several days previous to the races an unusual degree of bustle had prevailed at all the Inns and places of public entertainment in the neighbourhood, but on the morning of Thursday, accommodation could not be procured for one tenth part of the company who had come considerable distances to attend the races. A long line of road contiguous to the course was thronged with vehicles of all descriptions. On the course it was estimated that not less than six or seven thousand persons were assembled, and although the races are yet only in their infancy, a more brilliant display of fashionable, elegant, and highly respectable company was rarely witnessed.

The arrangements made for the accommodation of the company on the course reflect the greatest credit on the Noble Lord and the Hon. Baronet who officiated as stewards, as well as on the respectable gentlemen who acted as Clerks of the course; but the public were again especially indebted to John Button Esq. of Stiffords for his active exertions in promoting everything which could add to the interest of the races. On each side of the course, near the winning post and Stewards stations, wagons were placed to serve as stands for the company; most of them were filled with elegantly dressed females, but the grand focus of admiration was the wagon of Sir T.B. Lennard Bart., one of the Stewards, which was closely studded with clusters of female fashion and beauty who by the splendour of their dresses and brilliancy of their eyes gave a lustre to the picture which we have seldom seen surpassed even at Epsom, Ascot or Doncaster. We observed also other wagons on the course, where bright eyes and lovely faces, if not so numerous, shone at least as resplendently.

The first race, for the Ladies Cup, by ponies not exceeding eleven hands one inch created an intense degree of interest. Seven ponies started, but the contest laid entirely between Mr. Vidal's pony *Little Tommy*, (which has run every year since the establishment of the races), and Mr. Brown's grey pony *Riot*. The race was run in most beautiful style in two heats, and was very cleverly won by *Little Tommy* beating *Riot* by several lengths. The other ponies were so far behind that we did not notice the order in which they reached the post.

Workhouse arrangements and relief of the poor in both parishes have been noted earlier.

For the children in Rainham, besides three dames schools there was ,in 1833 a day school for 34 pupils, with an endowment for free education for 6 boys. This closed in '38, but a parochial school opened in 1846 with a master and a mistress.

In Wennington there was a day school with 27 children receiving free schooling and clothing.

Dagenham children had been smiled upon by dame fortune in the form of a wealthy farmer. In 1829, by the Will of William Ford, a trust fund of £10,000 - an incredibly large sum for those days - was set up to endow a school to educate boys and girls 'Along church principles'. By 1841 this had translated into a school and a teacher's house; and 30 boys aged 8 - 14, and 20 girls, aged 8 - 12 years were attending.

THE GOOD INTENT, RAINHAM.

Oldchurch Workhouse Opens.
The Railway Comes to Romford.
Running the Workhouse; Pauper Offences.

93

9. THE OLDCHURCH WORKHOUSE OPENS.

Sometime during the second week in the December of 1839 the two hundred and fifty or so inmates of the Barking House were moved to Romford - a considerable undertaking, including as it did many children and elderly and infirm paupers.

Surprisingly, no mention of it was made as such in the Minutes of the Board; neither is anything revealed by a careful search of the columns of the Chelmsford Chronicle of the time.

They, and their belongings, together with many beds and bedding, cooking and eating utensils, and scores of day to day items must have been trundled up the turnpike road to pour through the Oldchurch Workhouse gates by the cartload.

All that there is to signify that the move had taken place is that the Barking weekly accounts of £80.10.4d, for 10th. December for provisions and maintenance for 233 inmates proved to be the very last such entry; and the following week, 17th. December, the sum of £102.16.5d. for 271 inmates, was likewise the very first such entry in the New Workhouse accounts.

One thing is certain, the paupers and their belongings had not been moved by rail, even though the railway ran literally along the bottom of the Oldchurch grounds to terminate at the station then situated at the side of, and accessed from Waterloo road. The ten and a half miles of track, stretching from Dog Row, Mile End, to Romford, had been opened with much pomp and ceremony on the previous 18th. June, the second anniversary of queen Victoria's accession to the throne.

The original prospectus had appeared in 1834, and the

ADVERTISEMENT IN THE CHELMSFORD CHRONICLE, FRIDAY 14TH. JUNE 1839.

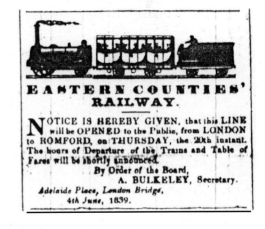

EASTERN COUNTIES' RAILWAY.

NOTICE IS HEREBY GIVEN, that this LINE will be OPENED to the Public, from LONDON to ROMFORD, on THURSDAY, the 20th instant. The hours of Departure of the Trains and Table of Fares will be shortly announced.

By Order of the Board,
A. BULKELEY, Secretary.

Adelaide Place, London Bridge,
4th June, 1839.

Grand Eastern Counties Railway was incorporated by Act of Parliament in 1836 with an authorised capital of £1,600,000. There were stations at Stratford and Ilford, with a railway works at Stratford. Another works opened in 1843 at Squirrels Heath, but its engineering side was transferred to Stratford later, leaving behind just the manufacture of sacks and tarpaulins.

On the inaugural day two trains each with fifteen coaches packed with all manner of dignitaries made their way to Romford. The ambassador of Persia, replete with ceremonial robes and jewelled sword, was among the guests. He arrived late, missed the train, and ordered his coachman to gallop down the turnpike road to Stratford. This he did, arriving in time for the ambassador to board the train there.

Crowds gathered to wave and cheer all along the length of the line. The reporter of the Chelmsford Chronicle wrote:- *'Romford it seems will be the principle point of attraction, as several gentlemen of high rank are expected to accompany the Directors down, and a cold collation served by Messrs. Bleadon & Co. is to be provided for 400 persons at the Barrack Ground.* (The same Barrack Field as was later built on to become 'New Romford') *The Company have concluded arrangements with Mr. French, the coachmaster at Chelmsford, for him to run a coach twice a day reaching Romford as the train starts for London, so that this will immediately throw open a more speedy mode of communication to the Metropolis. The whole distance from Chelmsford to the station at Mile End will be performed in two hours and a half. From Mile End omnibuses will be ready to convey passengers to any part of the Metropolis for 6d. The fares will be First Class 7/6d, Second Class 5/-'*

One cannot help but admire the commercial opportunism of the Chelmsford coachmaster in organising this coach/train

The train fares from Romford were:-

First Class;   2/6d.
Second Class: 1/6d.
Third Class: 1/-d.

The journey time was 29 minutes.

Oldchurch Workhous Opens.
The Railway Comes to Romford.
Running the Workhouse; Pauper Offences

95

link up right from day one. On the other hand he had to act
whilst he could; it would be only two years or so before the
railway came all the way to the County Town and foreclosed
on that aspect of his business.

Seven trains a day ran in each direction, ranging from nine
o'clock in the morning to seven in the evening. Despite the
high fares, the journey was popular and the total number of
passengers from the day it opened to 1st. December was given
as 49,001.

The line was extended back to Webbs Square, Shoreditch,
and out, first to Brentwood, then by March '43 to Colchester;
but not without a few problems. Timber viaducts had to be
erected over gaps in the embankment at Shenfield and Mount-
nessing, and there was an extensive landslip at Lexden where
60,000 cubic yards of earth were tipped into a space 30 yards
by 40 yards without increasing the height or width of the embankment one foot!

The final cost of the line from Shoreditch to Colchester was
£2,784,990., of which nearly a million pounds was spent on
legal matters relating to land compensation and other expenses
not actually included in the cost of the line itself. Lack of
Capital, originally obtained by subscription to £25 and £50
bonds, many of which were taken up by Liverpool merchants,
prevented the plan being carried out to extend the line as far as
Norwich and Yarmouth. In 1848 the railway crashed finan-
cially and was later amalgamated in 1862 with The Eastern Union, The Norfolk, The East Anglian, and The Newmarket railways to form the Great Eastern Railway.

Judging by the number of railway accidents eagerly reported in the Chelmsford Chronicle, literally from anywhere in
the country, there was a sizeable portion of the public who
viewed this new, excessively fast mode of transport with some
concern. Enthusiasm on the part of the drivers caused a few

minor shunting mishaps on our line, with a fatality on the very second day, when a train was derailed at Bow, allegedly doing 60mph., the driver and the fireman both being killed.

The Romford Board of Guardians crossed swords with the Railway Authority just once. Early in June, whilst finishing touches were being put to the line and station, a man called Akers was brought into the Workhouse with a broken thigh, sustained in the course of his work on the railway. After making application, the Board received a letter from Eastern Counties Railway saying: *'They did not feel authorised under the provisions of the Railway Act to enter into arrangements for the indemnity of the parishes against the casualties occasioned by the railway works'*.

Whereupon it was ordered that the relief given to Akers, a parishioner of Romford, be chargeable to Romford, and to be considered as a loan. (ie. ultimately repayable by him.)

The Board had other fish to fry. Its main task was to establish the smooth running of the Oldchurch Workhouse, with many loose ends to be tied up.

The remaining £1700 worth of Exchequer Bills were sold off to help settle outstanding accounts. It was agreed to buy the remainder of the land on which the Workhouse stood, Colonel Graves being willing to sell at £120 an acre.

A deputation of Guardians was sent to Jonathan Miles asylum in Hoxton to check on the state of the Union's lunatics housed there.

Mr. Miller, the master of the old Romford House, was paid off, together with his gratuity of £25 for services rendered over the years. Mrs. Taylor, the old matron, was likewise paid off.

The Commissioners made an order for a survey plan of Upminster.

Mr. Parson's bill for £2.16.0d for shaving the old men at Barking for the last quarter, was paid.

Oldchurch Workhouse Opens.
The Railway Comes to Romford.
Running the Workhous; Pauper Offences.

97

Four tenders to auction off the Romford House were submitted.

The Board accepted Mr. Collis' offer, in which he undertook:-

    To sell the property in lots.
    To post 400 bills.
    To advertise in 3 County and 2 London papers, twice.
    To print 200 catalogues and lithographic plans of the
        ground.

His charge for the above, plus his services to be £20.0.0d.

Regarding the old Barking House, the grounds were let out in the form of allotments to 'industrious cottagers'. However, in the opinion of the Vestry, several had not cultivated their land and were ordered to give up possession in one week. Others, not properly entitled to hold an allotment, were told to quit at Michaelmas next.

The Royal Exchange Assurance Co. agreed to insure the now occupied Union House at 1/6d. Per £100 excluding any part in which cotton, flax, or oakum picking was worked. The bill was as follows:-

    Total of buildings valued (by them) at £7,300.
    Of which £6,800 at 1/6d: £5. 2.0d
            £500 " 2/6d: 12.6d
                               £5.12.6d
    Plus Duty: £10.19.0d !!
                              £16.13.6d.

Two other matters hove into view. We might think of the Child Protection Agency as an innovation of our time; not so, it was up and running well in 1840, witness these two cases:-

The first concerns a girl called Lucy Young, who charged William Vinton of Rainham with being the father of her bastard child, now chargeable to the parish. Confirmatory evidence having been obtained, an application to the Justices at

Brentwood was made for an Order of Affiliation.

The second was made against Daniel Byford of South Weald, by Sarah Crow who, like Lucy Young had come to the Workhouse in her misfortune, to have her baby.

He was similarly charged, and both had Maintenance Orders taken out against them for a sum not exceeding 2/- per week, towards the upkeep of the children.

In the House, with the worsening winter weather and the scarcity of agricultural work, the numbers of paupers increased with each succeeding week, climbing steadily from 324 on the last day of December, first to 370, then 393, then 400 in mid February.

On admission, in accordance with the long standing insistence of the Commissioners, the inmates were divided into one of the following categories:-

> The aged and infirm, partly or wholly disabled.
> Orphans, foundlings, and children of widows remarried.
> Illegitimate children without their mothers.
>   "   "   with   "   "   .
> Women whose husbands are transported or who
> have deserted them.
> Insane, lunatics and idiots.
> Able-bodied, suffering sickness or accident.
>   "   "   out of work for other causes.

The sexes at all ages were strictly segregated, and except for very young children and their mothers, the categories were kept apart at all times save possibly for Sunday church, which must have been hard for whole families to endure.

The children attended school under the teachers.

The men worked growing vegetables in the garden, tending the pigs, manning the pump, picking oakum, working the mill for bruising oats, or working the corn mill - of which more later. They were under the direction of the Miller and Yardsman.

Oldchurch Workhouse Opens.
The Railway Comes to Romford.
Running the Workhouse, Pauper Offences.

99

The women were organised by the Mistress aided by the nurse
and the cook, to do the washing and cooking and cleaning, and
caring for the sick and the aged; which category accounted for
about half of the inmates.
Working parties were sent out to local farms in the season.

Paupers, on application, could go out to look for work. It
wasn't a prison, even if it felt like it; after all, the whole idea
was to encourage the inmates to go back to work in preference
to the conditions in the Workhouse.

Feeding, as with every other aspect of Workhouse life, was
subject to strict economy and the Dietaries were set out in detail. They could not be changed without the permission of the
Commissioners, and the paupers when they moved from the
old Houses no doubt brought their Dietaries with them. The
following is the Dietary from Barking:-

Breakfast: Men   6oz. bread and 1½pints gruel. Every day.
          Women 5oz.   "   " 1½pints " .   "   "

Dinner: Both men and women:
        Sun. Tues. Thurs. 5oz. cooked meat, 1lb. Potatoes.
        Mon. Wed. Sat.   1½ pints soup.
        Friday: Men: 14oz. rice or suet pudding.
          Women: 12oz. " " "   "

Supper: Sun. Tues. Thurs. 6oz. bread, 1½pints broth.
        the women: 5oz. bread "   "   "
       Mon. Wed. Fri.   6oz. bread, 2oz. cheese.
        and Sat.
        the women: 5oz. bread
Old people over 60 years may be allowed 1oz. Tea, 5oz. butter
And 7oz. sugar per week in lieu of gruel for breakfast.
Children under 9 years, diet at discretion, over 9 years, diet as
for women.

Sick to be dieted as directed by the \medical Officer.

It was a long break between supper and breakfast and the paupers used to keep back some of their bread. Matron found out and was told to collect up any uneaten bread after each meal, and to prohibit the bringing of bags or baskets to meals. To prevent hiding bread, all the cupboards in the day rooms were removed, and the bread which had started to be given with the soup at dinner on Monday, Wednesday and Saturday was also stopped. Harsh dealings.

Oh, and whilst they were about it, a proper vessel for brewing tea - for those allowed it - was to be installed in the kitchen.

Along list of items were put out to tender every Quarter. Amongst those accepted in March 1840 were:-

Milk:	8d. a gallon.	Potatoes:	£4 a ton.
Flour:	53/- a sack.	Quartern loaf:	7d
Cheese:	49/- a Cwt.	Beer.	30/- a barrel.
Tea:	5/- a lb.	Irish butter:	88/- a Cwt.
Sugar:	65/4d a Cwt.		

Then there were domestic items like coals: 26/- a ton, candles: 6/3d per 12 lb., and soap: 48/- per Cwt.

For the Board, to ease them through the strain of their weekly meetings there was wine at 42/- a dozen. They usually got through about four dozen bottles a Quarter.

Clothing was another sizeable account; Mr. Wilford, Mr. Lunn, and Mr. Smith, drapers all, were paid between them £100.11.0d for the Quarter ending 31st. March '40, not to mention £116.16.6d. To Mr. Lunn for blankets.

Other payments included £4.14.0d for trenchers (wooden plates), and £9.13.6d. To Mr. Ellis for mops and brooms; and £8.1.0d to Mr. Wood for leather for boot repairs.

Buried amongst all the others, were two interesting items that cropped up in the Quarterly accounts, unobtrusively

Oldchurch Workhouse Opens.
The Railway Comes to Romford.
Running the Workhouse, Pauper Offences.

101

throwing light on a previous problem. They were:-
To Mr. White for carriage of paupers and removing goods:
£13.10.0d.
The other one read: To Mr. Boyce for carriage of paupers:
14/6d.   It was by horse and cart then.

The Old Romford Workhouse was sold off in nine lots for a grand total of £862, or £815.1.0. nett after deductions including yet another Duty, this time of £20.14.0 , payable on the auction.

At this time other matters were settled. A cheque for £1000 was paid on the outstanding Builders account at the end of March, then £600 in May, and a payment of £1053.11.6d to the East of England Bank on 9th. June finally closed what had become a most troublesome account.

It was decided to run hot water to the girls wash house, and Mr. Whitaker, the plumber was paid £4.17.9d. To lay on the necessary pipes.

A boy complained of being kicked by the schoolmaster, who was accordingly reprimanded and ordered to keep a book of punishments in future.

The Medical Officer was asked to enter observations and suggestions in his weekly register with regard to the general management of the Workhouse. This he did, including one concerning the infirmary: *'Certain articles* (one wonders what?) *for use in the infirmary to be provided immediately'*

The Chaplain spent £3.9.3d. on books presumably for the children, and asked for a further £10 *'For books for the poor'*.

At one meeting, the architect, Mr. Edwards, presented the Board with two sets of framed plans of the Workhouse.

Even the Workhouse itself was rated to pay Poor Rate at 3d. In the pound on £224, and a cheque for £2.16.0 was paid to the Romford Overseers of the Poor.

It was decided to build a new fire engine house consequent

on the sale and demolition of the old Workhouse, in whose grounds the old building had stood.

In this manner the day to day, week to week, month by month business of the Board of Guardians took shape, Things were never in danger of becoming a dull routine; a constant stream of incidents saw to that.

Towards the end of 1841 the ten year Census figures had to be collected, another of those extra jobs that the Board had taken on, including apportioning the cost of the exercise between the individual parishes. The new population total for the Union was 21,693, an increase over the 1831 census of 1172, or about 6%.

Mr. Roper, one of the two bakers who supplied bread for Outdoor Relief, was a constant source of complaint; if the loaves weren't underweight, then they went mouldy with monotonous regularity. Mind you, only one delivery was made a week, and he had a point when he suggested making two deliveries; as he reminded members of the Board, would the loaves in their larders remain fresh for seven days?

Petty misdemeanours by the paupers cropped up regularly; 1842 seemed to be a year full of recalcitrance:-

24th. May, *'It appearing in the pauper offence book that the following boys, namely;-*

John Hammond	*aged 9*	*William Cater*	*aged 10*
Enoch Walker	*" 9*	*William Haslam*	*" 12*
David Simpson	*" 10*		

Had been flogged on the 21st. with a birch rod for throwing stones on the 20th. instant, they were brought before the Board when the punishment was approved of.'

Again, from the pauper offence book;-

'14th. June, William Oliver, locked up for six hours with bread and water for supper, for striking Thomas Elliot'.

The same day, John Ryland and William Holdgate were

The Board that day consisted of Messrs. Bearblock, Cove, Freeman, Pemberton, Choat, Parker, Brittain, Tabrum, Lee, Tolbut, Macarthy, and Gutteridge. Twelve good men and true, none of whom had ever in his youth so far departed from the path of righteousness as to throw stones.

Oldchurch Workhouse Opens.
The Railway Comes to Romford.
Running the Workhouse; Paupers Offences.

103

charged with smoking in the hall. Ryland denied the charge, but it was admitted by Holdgate. *'It appearing to have been inadvertently done, no punishment was awarded'.*

5th. July: William Hill, for going out and getting very drunk on 28th. June, was punished by locking up for 24 hours and keeping him on bread and water.
Also William Prestlove, for absenting himself from the House last Sunday, without leave, had his meat stopped for one day..

2nd. August: Samuel Cook, 13 years, Joseph Littleford, 13 years, William Haslam (again), 12 years, Enoch Walker (also again), 9 years, *'Were reported as having been guilty of throwing stones and other ungovernable conduct on 27th. July last, as having been punished by a good flogging with a small hazel stick. The boys being brought before the Board, were admonished by the Chairman, and the punishment approved of'.*

13th. Sept. *'The Master, having reported that John Cartwright, who had leave of absence on Monday 5th., to return the same evening, was brought home late on Tuesday night in a state of intoxication by a policeman, and had been kept in the probationary ward until the following night upon bread and water'.*

The same day: *'Thomas Scarborough, 10 years, Henry Hicks, 9 years, Thomas Mills, 8 years, Jacob Piercy 7 years, and Ambrose Piercy 12 years were reported as having been well flogged with a birch, the first four for misconduct in the chapel, and the last for swearing'.*

Ambrose Piercy, and another boy, George Ashman, aged 15 years, decided to make a dash for it. They were reported as having made their escape over the wall on the evening of 15th. September, and they were brought back about 2 o'clock the next day by the Beadle of Mile End. The Board ordered them to be locked up during the play hours for the next two days and to have bread and gruel only for the next two days.

And so it went on, until a couple of days after Christmas when general revolt seemed to be in the air:-
John Brown, 16 years, admonished for refusing to work and for smoking.
Charles Vinton, Elijah Walker, John Reed and John Maskell, for playing cards on two days, no meat on Sunday and Thursday next.
And yet another list of miscreants:-

Charles Vinton.	For refusing to work the pump on the
Isaac Spooner.	23rd. and on the 24th., and for making
Christopher Hunt.	a noise, likewise to have their meat
Edward Hawkins.	stopped on Sunday and Thursday next.
John Sidd.	Vinton and Spooner to be taken before
Edward Newman.	The Magistrates for punishment as
Charles Clarks.	refractory paupers.
William Bishops.	

The Board further ordered that no tobacco be allowed in the House, except that issued by the Master.

In the January of 1842 the Chairman of the Board Mr. Pearce, J.P., died. The vice Chairman, Mr. Bearblock was elected in his place, and from among the Guardians Charles Cove, the Hornchurch builder, became the new vice chairman.

At a meeting on 1st. March a paragraph from the Essex and Herts. Mercury was read to the Board:-
'Many people think that the Board have not made a very judicious choice in the person of their vice Chairman, they might have selected one with more feelings to the poor'.

Predictably, the Board closed ranks and proposed a vote of confidence in Mr. Cove; and that *'They unite in bearing testimony to his kindly treatment of the poor, and in expressing their regret at the publication of the portion of the paragraph relating to him'.*

Very few paupers would have been able to read or write,

Oldchurch Workhouse Opens.
The Railway Comes to Romford.
Running the Workhouse; Pauper Offences.

105

or so much as been able to afford a newspaper, yet they would have been the section of the community most disturbed to learn of Mr. Cove's appointment. One wonders who indeed did communicate with the newspaper, and to what extent his appointment accounted for the continual discontent in the House over the previous twelve months.

However, elections for the Board were held annually in March, and when the 1843 results were declared, and a new Chairman and vice Chairman elected, it transpired that although Mr. Cove had been returned unopposed by the rate paying parishioners of Hornchurch, unlike the Chairman, he had not been re-appointed vice Chairman. By a unanimous vote of the Guardians, his place was taken by James Paulin Esq., of Aldborough Hatch. Belatedly, the Board had got the message.

It was decided to enlarge the Workhouse mill by adding a dressing machine, and Mr. Carter, the millwright was asked to prepare an estimate. Advertisements for a Superintendent of Labour and Mill Manager were placed, and three weeks later the job was offered to Thomas Warden at a salary of £20 a year with board and double rations. The mill alterations went ahead and 6 Quarters of best red wheat were ordered *'To be delivered at the Union House this coming week'*.

There were two sacks to a Quarter, and a sack of wheat weighed 2¼cwt., so 6 Qtrs. weighed 27 Cwt. This was wheat for milling and sale as top grade flour. For baking bread in the House 'seconds' were used.

A month later, 12 sacks 2½bushels, of flour were sold for £21.17.6d.

In those days flour was measured by volume, and a sack of flour contained 4 bushels or 16 pecks or 32 gallons, and it actually weighed 2 cwt;, which is why, in the good old days when you went to the grocers you were sold a bag of flour weighing 3½lbs., that weight being equal to half a gallon.

It wasn't all bad news however. The Board quite liked to give praise where praise was due. Miss Pepper, the girls' schoolteacher of some years standing, was their target in the summer of '42. At the meeting on 14th June they recorded *'That this Board highly appreciating the services of Miss Pepper, schoolmistress of the Romford Union from its formation, present her with a gratuity of Ten Pounds. They cannot express too high an opinion of her attention to the general duties of her appointment and her kind and able treatment of the children, as evidenced by their excellent demeanour and their advancement in learning'*.

Miss Pepper's salary was £20 a year, with board and lodging.

Today, you are sold 1.5 Kilos of flour, which is a messy 3.3lbs.,or short weight for 3½lb. - it is called progress.

The original 27cwt. of wheat cost £14.18.0d., and had produced 25cwt. of flour sold at £21.17.6d., showing a profit of £7.9.6d. - over 50%, and that didn't include the sale of pollard (middlings), and bran, the bye products of the milling process. Clearly, this was a successful operation, and it was pursued with vigour. From now on wheat was bought and flour was sold every three or four weeks.

The Workhouse Master suggested a second pair of stones be added to the mill. This was agreed, the Board insisting that French burr stones be installed. The millwright undertook the work for £38.8.0d, *'if the flywheel be dispensed with'*.

This mill for grinding corn was in addition to the one for bruising oats, and like it, was worked, through a system of gearing by cranking handles. Two pairs of stones would have taken a lot of turning, and was actually worked by teams of twelve paupers, six on each turning handle.

In January, '44 the Miller and Yardsman resigned and his place was taken by Henry Glasspool, aged 24 years. At the same time it was ordered that each person be required to work at the mill for one hour before, and one and a half hours after breakfast between Michaelmas and Lady day; and for two hours before breakfast, between Lady day and Michaelmas, *' provided that such amount of work shall not be required from any person whose age or strength or capacity it shall appear not to be suited'*. This order was directed at the ever increasing number of vagrants who now sought overnight shelter and breakfast before moving on. If provision for the paupers worked out on average at 6d. a day, no more than half that amount was to be spent on feeding the tramps.

To accommodate the tramps overnight, arrangements had been made to use the stables.

Emigration.
The Pitcairn Scandal.
The Failure of Johnsons Bank.

107

10.   PAUPER EMIGRATION.

Canada, Australia and New Zealand in the second quarter of the nineteenth century were crying out for immigrants; women as well as men - in fact there was a real shortage of marriageable women. Agents in Britain placed tempting advertisements in the papers, offering jobs galore in every trade and occupation at wages three, four and five times those obtainable here. They circularised the Union Workhouses too offering through the Guardians a chance of a fresh start and a rosy future for those who were willing to take the plunge.

The Romford Union was no exception, and on 7th. May, '44 the Minutes recorded that *'A gentleman from the offices of Messrs. Marshall & Co. having attended to explain the terms upon which they are willing to convey immigrants to Quebec, namely for £5.7.6d. each besides bedding and clothing, the following women, who had expressed a desire to emigrate were called in, namely:-*

Elizabeth Bridge, belonging to Barking.
Mary Green,   "   "   ".
Eliza Hammond,   "   " Romford.
Maria Smith,   "   " Dagenham.
Mary Bateman,   "   " Upminster.

The Chairman told them that on landing at Quebec they would receive £1 each and that the Govt. Agent would look after them for ten days, after which they would have to provide for themselves.

Elizabeth Bridge, being a married woman, was told by the Board that they could not send her without her husband. Mary Green declined to go to Quebec, but the others, expressing a strong desire to go, the Clerk was directed to write to the

44

A LIST OF ARTICLES,

NECESSARY TO AN EMIGRANT, FOR THE

CULTIVATION OF FIFTY ACRES AND UPWARDS,

PARTLY GRASS, PARTLY ARABLE LAND.

THE under-mentioned Goods have been supplied by MARY WEDLAKE & CO. to parties who have sailed in the following ships for Port Natal—*Alliwal, Sovereign, Edward,* and the *Lady Bruce.* They have for the last twenty years supplied Settlers to Swan River, Melbourne, and Adelaide, and all the Australian Colonies.

Persons becoming purchasers may have the benefit of an introduction to any parties in either of the above Colonies.

A Scotch Cart, fitted complete, from £12 12s. to £18 18s.
A Set of Irons, complete, for a Scotch Cart
A Plough, to order, fitted with Wheel and Coulter, from £2 12s. 6d. to £4 5s.
Iron ditto, from £4 10s. to £5 10s.
1 Set Plough Whipple Trees
2 Dozen Shares
1 Wrought Share
2 Light Harrows and Weigh Tree
1 Chaff Cutter, or Box, from £1 10s. to £7 7s.
1 Scarifier from £2 15s. 6d. to £10 10s.
Half-dozen Cotton Hoes, 8-inch
COTTON GINS
50 Strong Harrow Tines, and Iron Work complete for 2 Strong Harrows
52 Harrow Tines for a gang of 4 light seed Harrows, and Weigh Tree for same
A Circular Pig Trough
Wheel Barrow, Shifting, from £1 10s. to £2 2s.
Half-dozen No. 2 Shovels
Half-dozen No. 2 Spades
Half-dozen Potato Forks
Half-dozen Pick-Axes
3 Pairs Chain Traces
A Set of strong Cart Harness
6 Ox Yokes and Bows
Ox Ties, half-dozen
Half-dozen Sickles
Half-dozen Bill-Hooks
Half-dozen Scythes
6 Pair Bullock Chains
A Dressing Machine, from £7 10s. to £12 12s.
A Pole Iron and Nuts
Weeding Forks, 1 dozen
Hammers, sorted, 1 dozen
Port Natal or New Zealand Hatchets
Axes
Mattocks
Hoop Iron
Rubbers
West Indian Hoes
Tents, according to size, from £3 to £20
Iron Houses, from 120 guineas to £300
Portable Forges, from £3 3s. to £5 5s.

And various other Articles, supplied at a few hours' notice.
(The above are indispensable to a Colonist.)

Farmers too, were emigrating; as this enterprising list of farm tools, produced by Wedlakes, illustrates.

Poor Law Commissioners for the authority to raise the necessary funds.

Again, the following May, '*A person named John Smith, shipping agent of 37, Betts Street, St. George's in the East, applied to the Board to allow the undermentioned men to go out to Sidney on the convict ship Marion, now about to sail, namely:- William Holdgate, John Goddard, Sam Cook, and John Mead belonging to Barking, Charles Clark of Rainham,, and George Ashman of Upminster. The men being called in, severally expressed their willingness to go, whereupon the Board agreed, provided the enquiries the Chairman undertook to make into the chartacter of the applicant and the owners of the ship proved satisfactory, to supply the necessary outfit, namely £5.10.0. for each man, to include a payment of £1 upon his landing'.*

Then it was the turn of a man from Barking named Bertie, he was funded to the sum of £7, and three weeks later Isaac Herrington of Hornchurch and W.H.Westwood from Dagenham in the sum of £3.0.6d. each, with an additional charge of 11/- and 6/- respectively for conveyance to Deptford.

In this manner emigration proceeded.

In the general rebelliousness of the previous year, things were pretty unruly in the classroom too. '*The Board having taken into consideration the report of the Chaplain and the Visiting Committee as to the state of the boys school, requested the Chaplain to prepare a plan for the education and industrial training of the boys, and to report the same at the next meeting*'

In its anxiety to cut costs to the bone, the Board failed in the main to attract any but the poorest grade of schoolteachers. Miss Pepper had resigned to go to look after her sick and ageing father, and in the general change round a Mr. And Mrs. James Pitcairn were appointed schoolteachers.

Emigration.
The Pitcairn Scandal.
The Failure of Johnsons Bank.

109

'They were informed that their eldest child would not be per-mitted to come, but that they might bring their youngest, three years old, but no rations would be allowed for it'.

Then, the following March, came the devastating entry in the Minutes:-

'It having been represented to the Board that Mr. Pitcairn, the schoolmaster of the Union had grossly misconducted himself, and the Board having made a full investigation into the circum-stances of the case resolved forthwith to dismiss Mr. Pitcairn from the appointment held by him. The Board also resolved that they could not consistently retain the services of Mrs. Pit-cairn the schoolmistress in consequence of the misconduct of her husband and they determined also that she should be dis-missed from the situation held by her in the establishment'.

And went they did. Adverts. were placed, applicants inter-viewed, and successors appointed, albeit on probation for one month.

Six weeks later came a solicitors letter claiming one Quarter's back pay on Mrs. Pitcairn's salary. Their contract probably said that each side should give three months notice or forfeit the Quarter's salary, and technically Mrs. Pitcairn had not been dismissed for any misdemeanour.

Another six weeks went by then a letter arrived from the Poor Law Commissioners enclosing a second letter from James Pit-cairn preferring charges against the Guardians and some of the Officers of the Union.

Mr. Pitcairn had been dismissed with ignominy; now he wasn't going to be able to get another teaching job anywhere easily, and he wasn't going to go without taking a swipe at the Rom-ford Union.

The Board wrote back to the Commissioners:-

'With respect to the first portion of the charge against the Mas-ter, that of drunkenness, the Guardians have interrogated

strictly the Porter of the Union with the view of ascertaining if at any time the Master has been admitted into the House in a state of inebriety, but this was distinctly denied by him; and as the Master is unable to gain access to the House without the knowledge of the Porter the Guardians consider his testimony upon the subject, which they see no reason whatever to impugn completely negatives the assertion of Pitcairn'.

There was a lot more in this vein, including charges against the Matron , Mrs. Sellars:- *'Several of the girls do however do knitting, but only for their own amusement, and never for longer than two hours'.*

The Guardians refuted all of Pitcairn's charges and their letter finally concluded:-

'The Guardians wish to refrain from observing upon the motives which it is evident to them have influenced Pitcairn in preferring these charges against themselves and the Officers of the Union, and that they have merely in conclusion to add that they have felt some difficulty in replying to several of the charges from their very general nature. But the Guardians will be happy to furnish the Commissioners with any further information they may require, feeling satisfied that such charges are unfounded and that they will bear the test of strict investigation'. And there the matter ended.

The failure of Johnson's Bank in June 1844 was however the scandal that caused the biggest outrage. It came as a shock to the whole community, the more so by the timing of the announcement; and it was a bitter revelation to the Board, for Johnson's acted in the capacity of Treasurer to the Union.

Wednesday 5th. June had been just another busy market day in Romford. Farmers and dealers had bought and sold, and there had been much talk of the recent rains which had broken the long and damaging drought of the Spring of that year. Money had changed hands, had been deposited and withdrawn,

Emigration.
The Pitcairn Scandal.
The Failure of Johnson's Bank.

111

had been taken home in the wallets of the bank's customers, much of it in the form of Johnson's own £5 notes, for like other country banks they were free to print their own.

The following day, Thursday, the bank failed to open its doors. It wasn't the first bank to have failed. Back in 1826 The Romford Agricultural Bank had been forced to close following a disastrous run on its resources. That had occurred at a time when similar panic demands on their liquidity had led to a nationwide crop of failures among the country banks of the time.

No general air of financial crisis pervaded the scene in 1844; no hint of trouble to come. One can imagine the anger and resentment. Why, asked the furious citizens of Romford, had the bank opened on the Wednesday, the town's busiest day, when they must have known that their enterprise was on the point of collapse?

FACSIMILE OF A FIVE POUND NOTE
AS ISSUED BY JOHNSONS BANK.

The Sun, a London evening paper, caught the public mood when it reported '*Many cases of very great hardship have caused a feeling anything but favourable to the partners of the bank, and the keeping open the last market day, to close the following morning has been very freely commented upon*'.

The news spread fast. Elizabeth Ann Branfill wrote in her diary for that day '*Romford bank broke. Went there in the gig to hear*'. She lived with her husband at Upminster Hall. Her husband had served as a captain in the 3rd. Regiment of

Dragoons during the Peninsular War, and had fought at Waterloo. He had retired from the army to become Deputy Lieutenant of Essex, and a Justice of the Peace. He was at this time seriously ill and confined to bed. He died on 7th. October, leaving his wife who, on account of his long illness had already taken up the reins to manage the estate with its numerous staff. She also had a son, splendidly named Champion Branfill.

Of course, the reason for staying open on the Wednesday was plain to all. *'When the Bankruptcy Court messenger took possession of the bank with books and property at Romford'* Stated the Chelmsford Chronicle of 14th. June, *'He found less than £1000 in cash, and also about £9,000 in their own notes. The balance in hand on Wednesday night appeared to have been about a £1000 more than it would have been had the bank closed on Wednesday morning instead of Thursday'.*

Small though the bank was, with its single branch, its depositors were drawn from quite a large area. Several lived in Grays, where the loss by notes held and by deposit accounts was reckoned to be not less than £5,000. One such man was John Meason, lime burner of that town. From other districts came men like Thomas Woodfine the Hornchurch brewer; and John Cooper, miller West Ham, and Harvey George, the auctioneer, who came from Ilford, and who stood to lose £4,000.

Among farmers there was Thomas Waters, tenant farmer of Little Mollands Hall, South Ockendon. He wrote to his landlord, John Oxley Parker, for advice and help. *'I have by me £50 which I put in the bank for payment of the laborers (sic) and other sundry expenses. Which I hope you will do what you can for me to remedy this evil as I am fearful the dividend will be small'.*

Oxley Parker, writing from home at Woodham Mortimer Hall replied: *'I doubt whether it will be in my power to render you any assistance, but should I have the opportunity of doing*

Emigration.
The Pitcairn Scandal.
The Failure of Johnson's Bank.

113

you any service I assure you that I will not fail to take advantage of it. I will thank you in future to put any monies you may have in hand on account of the farming a/c. to my credit at Messrs. Sparrow & Co., bankers at Chelmsford'.

Oxley Parker's account with Johnson's Bank had previously stood at £650, but on 27th. May, just ten days before the failure, he had by good fortune drawn a cheque for £250, marked 'Pay self at Sparrow & Co.'

As regards the paper money in circulation, one newspaper described it as *'A very general distribution of the notes, which almost every farmer selling produce at Romford market took home with him. The notes are freely offered at 2/6d in the pound, and no buyers'.*

Sadly, The Bank Charter Act, which authorised precisely what each bank's total of notes was to be henceforth, did not become law until 19th. July, 1844, that is, six weeks too late to be of any help.

A meeting of the creditors was held at the White Hart Inn, Romford, and a committee which included Mr. Woodfine, Harvey George, Mr. Cooper and Mr. Meason ,was formed to represent their interests .

As for the Board of Guardians, their account stood at £664.13.7d., and they immediately applied for re-imbursement of the money. Solicitors on behalf of Thomas Johnson wrote back suggesting that the wisest course would be *'To prove the debt under a fiat of bankruptcy next Monday, rather than commit an old man of almost eighty years to prison - assuming any J.P. could be found willing to do such a thing'.*

A letter to Mr. Johnson junior, written by Edmund Griffin, the Board's Clerk (and an attorney) stated *'The refusal of Mr. Weston, I believe under your advice, to execute the Surety Bond, and his neglect to inform me of his objection has left the Union without security, and has exposed me to great censure'.*

The Board, which normally took so much care in these matters, had, by default, no Guarantor to fall back on. Mr. Weston, ostensibly the Guarantor, had been talked out of signing the Security Bond by Johnson Jnr. His reply consisted of a set of convoluted reasons for advising Weston not to sign, and finished by saying that he had seen his father '*Who was applying to his friends for assistance*'.

Poor Mr. Griffin took full responsibility for the omission, and wrote to the Poor Law Commission to that effect. All the same, it was the Board who instituted proceedings against Johnson's, and in the meantime Octavius Mashiter agreed to act as treasurer; and the manager of the recently opened Romford branch of the London and County Banking Co. undertook to make any advances that may be necessary in the circumstances, no doubt sensing a business opportunity.

The case made its way through the Bankruptcy Courts. The full name of the bank was Johnson, Johnson and Mann, and was described as drawing on Sir Richard Carr, Glynn & Co., and Whitmore Wells & Co. Presumably these merchant banker's names were intended to add a ring of security to the House. Thomas Johnson, who lived at Gaines Lodge, Upminster, was an Alderman of Portsoken Ward in the City of London. The Observer newspaper noted '*The name of Thomas Johnson, Alderman of Portsoken Ward, having appeared in the list of bankrupts, the citizens of London expect that the gown will be immediately resigned into the hands of the constituency*'.

He was personally overdrawn at his bank to the tune of £30,000.

The most unfortunate person in the whole case was the third partner, Charles Mann. He had first met Johnson senior when the latter came into his extensive oil and colour business in Aldgate in 1814 on the retirement of a previous partner.

Emigration.
The Pitcairn Scandal.
The Failure of Johnson's Bank.

115

Johnson, who had started up the bank in 1826 on his own, invited Mann to take a quarter share in the bank in 1831, to which he unfortunately agreed.

A sum of £65 was credited to him, but he never visited the bank or saw its books, or became aware of any of its affairs. The Court estimated liabilities of £60,000 against assets of a mere £2,500. However, all the assets of the owners had been seized (the laws of limited liability did not come in until 1855), and these included the Aldgate business, which after paying its own creditors twenty shillings in the pound, would realise a further £15,000 to £18,000.

Mann wrote to the Court apologising to the bank's creditors for its failure. His letter concluded '*For myself, my overconfidence has brought upon my family distress; has swept away the earnings of more than forty years of devoted, assiduous and untiring attention to a business upon which I had depended for support for myself and my wife in our old age, and a provision for my sons, one of whom has been fifteen years in the business. This is all lost to me, and I stand now before the world a ruined man*'.   Signed Charles Mann, Aldgate, 24th. June, 1844.

This statement brought profound sympathy for its writer, and if anything heightened the bitterness already felt for Thomas Johnson.

Harvey George, the Ilford auctioneer, who had been elected an assignee, exercised his right to cross examine Johnson: '*According to your account, I find that at the time of opening the bank you were £4526.2.6d in debt.*'

Mr. Johnson: '*I don't believe it, I was not insolvent at the time.*'

Mr. George: '*I want to know on what principle you went to Romford and opened the bank in 1826, when you were £4,000 worse than nothing?*'

After more of this, Mr. Commissioner Goulburn commented '*I do not think we shall profit by keeping up this examination. The question is whether the bankrupt has furnished the
best account in his power. As to his general conduct as a
trader, when he comes up for his certificate* (of discharge from
bankruptcy) *he will have to answer for it.*'

The bankrupt was then declared to have passed his examination and the matter was at an end.

The final total dividend paid was 11/6d in the £1, and was a
good deal more than those angry creditors on that fateful
Thursday morning had ever dared to hope for.

The Publid Health Act and Cholera.
Workhouse to Infirmary.
The Hungry Forties.

117

11.   FROM WORKHOUSE TO INFIRMARY.

Out in the towns and villages of the Union changes were being made which would improve the general health of everyone. By the mid eighteen forties the Medical clubs were well established, and the treatment of the sick on Outdoor Relief via the Medical Officers was also working well generally.

Smallpox vaccination, free for all children, was growing in popularity. From 1843 details of the numbers vaccinated appear in the accounts of the Board, the doctors being reimbursed according to the number of patients treated; thus the figures for August '43 show a total of 394 for the whole of the Union.

In 1848 the Public Health Act was passed. It followed yet another massive report by Edwin Chadwick, published earlier in 1842, this time on 'The Sanitary Conditions of the Labouring Population'. Chadwick's work was based on information supplied by all the country's Poor Law physicians, including of course the seven Medical Officers of the Romford Union. Among other things, the Act empowered ordinary citizens to report rotting filth, blocked ditches, and anything they deemed to be a health hazard, and to insist that they be cleared upon pain of fines or worse.

Complaints followed thick and fast. The infamous Sun Yard had already been the subject of a note in the minutes of the Board of Guardians way back in February '43:
'The Board directed the Churchwardens and Overseers of Romford to cause all the rooms in the houses in Sun Yard to be limed white in the hope of stopping if possible the progress of the fever raging there'.

And again, three years later in March, '46:

'Mr. Curtis, bricklayer (his) bill for whitewashing rooms in Sun Alley, £3.17.0d.'

Both the above in response to outbreaks of cholera no doubt. Another entry, this one dated 25th. July '48 reads:-

'The Clerk was directed to take the instructions of Mr. Parker, the Relieving Officer, as to measures to be taken against certain owners and occupiers of the premises in Sun Yard, and other parties, for the nuisances existing there.'

The problem here was rotting offal and waste from a butchery in the yard.

Medical Officers, no doubt encouraged by having been called upon to contribute their observations to Mr. Chadwick's seminal report, were also anxious now to initiate proceedings themselves for the removal of hazards:

'Mr. Collins, one of the Medical Officers of the Union attended and laid before the Board a certificate in writing signed by himself and Mr. Bowers, surgeon, of the existence of an offensive drain in the town of Romford, and the Clerk was directed to lay a complaint before the Justices for the Liberty, against the owners and the occupiers of the premises, with a view to obtaining an Order from the Justices for cleansing the drain in question'

Member of the Board also took up the cudgels:

7th. November, '48:- Mr. Dunnett produced seven notices of *'offensive ditches and accumulations of filth'* which were injurious to the public health, all signed by himself and two other householders. A committee of four Guardians was set up to investigate, and they concurred with the notices.

Unfortunately, as if to underline the need to make every effort to improve sanitation, cholera again reached epidemic proportions in 1849, and the Guardians were issued with special forms form the General Board of Health upon which to make

The Public Health Act and Cholera.
Workhouse to Infirmary.
The hungry Forties.

119

returns of the number of persons 'Attacked by cholera and other epidemic diseases'. The disease was rife in the overcrowded centre of Barking and the inhabitants of Ilford ward, worried that it would spread to them, called a public meeting and elected a committee, 27 strong and including 4 of the 8 Guardians for Barking. They made formal application to have the committee recognised, to which the Guardians agreed, and resolved *'That such committee be authorised to fit up, should it become necessary, suitable rooms or places of refuge to which families of poor persons attacked by cholera, or necessitous persons living under the same roof or in the vicinity of the persons so attacked, may be removed. The such committee be also authorised to appoint an Inspector of Nuisances for Ilford and Chadwell Wards at such remuneration as they may deem sufficient for that purpose'.*

They appointed Mr. Cornelius Green for one year, to go round the Wards once a quarter and report the nuisances existing therein; his remuneration to be £1.1.0d per quarter.

Alongside this it was decided to enlarge the Workhouse infirmary, and Mr. Edwards the architect was called in and asked to prepare a plan for two additional wards for ten patients, each with *'Proper accommodation for nurses and other suitable officers'.*

Mr. Curtis and Mr. Hammond's tender at the sum of £330.10.0d was accepted, and construction went ahead. A first payment against work completed was made on 20th. June, '48, the second instalment on the 15th. August.

Tenders were put out for 20 iron bedsteads, 5 slate washing trays, and a 65 gallon washing copper. Bedsteads with six legs and sacking bottoms at 14/6d each, plus one 'Hospital bedstead with self acting back' at 22/- were bought in. The washing trays cost £6.10.0d fixed in, and the copper, 'with 30 lb. Extra weight thrown into the sides' came in at 12/- a lb., the old copper in exchange at 7/4d a lb.

By the end of October the work was complete and the wards were brought into use. In one sense, the Workhouse, with its aged and infirm, and the chronically sick making up a sizeable proportion of its inmates, had always been something of a hospital. Now, with these additional wards, it could be said to have embarked on the long journey which was to finally culminate in today's modern complex, leaving the erstwhile Workhouse itself standing dwarfed and overshadowed in a forgotten corner of the grounds.

These years were dubbed 'The Hungry Forties'. In many parts of the country they were dire indeed; trade was slow, there was recession and much hardship and poverty. Famine, and the potato blight had struck Ireland in 1845. Large parts of the English crop were affected too. 1846 saw no remission; blight and the weather took their toll of the crop. January and February in Essex were cold; March was very dry, and May was exceptionally wet. June and July were hot, and four inches of rain fell in August's thunderstorms, too late to fill out the parched potato crop but in good time to lay the ripening wheat -how much of it would have sprouted in the ear as it lay flattened in the mud?

Prices started to climb in '45; wheat, from 48/- a Quarter in the early part of the year to 62/- in October, then spiralling upwards throughout '46 to 73/- by January '47, and 77/- in March of that year, putting the price of a loaf up from 4½d to 8d. Potatoes rose to £5 a ton, then £7.10.0d, if available.

The Workhouse started buying in carrots at £3 a ton, - the old price of potatoes. The price of meat too, rose; even the legs and shins used for the inmates stew. By the middle of 1847 they were 50% dearer at 3/6d a stone (14lbs.).

For the parishes of the Romford Union it was a case of hunger in the real sense of the word, with calls on the Poor Rate to

The Public Health Act and Cholera.
Workhouse to Infirmary.
The Hungry Forties.

121

cover the third Quarter of the year up to a record £3805. Fortunate, what went up eventually came down again too, and by the early part of 1849 prices were approaching normal once again.

Cash, and the demand for cash was always at the heart of everything; but now, for the first time, Central Government was beginning to take a hand. The very earliest contributions had been the £23,000, nationwide for education in 1833. This annual sum rapidly increased, and when the Oldchurch House opened a contribution was made to the running of its classes for the boys and girls.

By 1848 the useful sum of £232.10.0d from the Paymaster of the Civil Service was received annually. The certificate of payment stated explicitly that the Parliamentary grant was to be, £30 towards the master's salary, and £12 for the mistress. The remainder of the money went towards the salaries of the Union's Medical Officers.

Concerned that the money should not be miss-applied, they sent inspectors round to assess and report on the conduct and the management of the schools. The first recorded visit I can find is for 19th. November, 1850, on which day the Auditors threatened to descend on the Workhouse.

Starting in 1846, a new demand for money from the parishes of the Romford Union began to be made. As usual, this was to be through the good offices of the Board, acting now increasingly in their fast emerging role of embryo Local Authority. This demand was for County and Police rates. Thus:-

10th. Feb. '46. *'Pursuant of the precept* (rate demand) *received of the Clerk of the Peace for the County, a cheque was given to T. Gepp Esq., deputy treasurer - County Rate £109.7.3d., Police Rate £146.9.7d.'*

The parishes were accordingly debited at ½d in the pound for the County Rate, and ¾d in the pound for the Police Rate.

Checking weights and measures would certainly have meant a visit to the new tenant of these premises once they were let:-

TO LET.

PUBLIC HOUSE, situate at Dagenham, near Romford, Essex, doing a beer trade of £30 a month, and a proportionate Spirit trade. The coming-in will be about £240.
For particulars apply to Mr. G. Collis, Auctioneer, Romford, Essex.

TYPICAL ADVERTISEMENT FROM THE FRONT PAGE OF THE CHELMSFORD CHRONICLE.

Not all the parishes however were liable. Romford, Hornchurch and Havering-atte-Bower were exempt the County Rate, presumably because they comprised the ancient Liberty of Havering; and Barking and Dagenham, coming as they did within the Metropolitan Police area, were exempt the Police Rate.

Early in 1850 a new item was added, namely a rate for the erection of a County Lunatic Asylum. This was the institution to be built the following year at Brentwood, and always to remain in the jurisdiction of the County.

The Police Rate was of course levied to cover the costs of the Essex Constabulary, founded in 1840. Three constables were initially allocated to Romford: one was Constable No. 45, James R. Barnard, another was Constable No. 17, Joseph Copsey, and the third was Constable No. 96, Frederick W. Lambert. There was no Police Station as such, the constables being billeted in local ale houses. By the end of March '41, they had been joined by Superintendent Anthony Martindale; and White's Directory for 1848 lists also John Hayden, Police Inspector, as living in Waterloo Road, which was on the New Romford estate referred to earlier. It should be said that at that time there was no intermediate rank of police sergeant.

The purposes to which the County Rate was put included items like officially checking the weights and measures of all the shops and traders. These were undertakings which had become additional responsibilities of the County Judiciary, much as the Romford Guardians had acquired responsibility for Census returns, Registration of Births, Marriages and Deaths etc. They were the outcome of Acts of Parliament which increasingly impinged directly on the lives of everyone, great and small.

Save for outright industrialisation, Romford, Barking, Dagenham and Hornchurch, together with the other parishes of the Union, constituted a microcosm of England and the English

The Public Health Act and Cholera.
Workhouse to Infirmary.
The Hungry Forties.

123

way of life in early Victorian times. And within that microcosm dwelt another microcosm, The Oldchurch Workhouse, reflecting unconsciously many facets of the lives of the Union's citizens, and all duly recorded in the neat copperplate pages of the Minutes of the Board of Guardians.

They ranged from the trivial to the tragic, from brave hope to despair, all jostling for attention, week upon hurrying week:-

There was an entry for the repair of a wooden leg: 4/10d.

Another, for the purchase of 'Best quill pens': 8/- a hundred.

And another, for printing 6 treasurer's Check (sic) Books, 200 leaves in each: 14/6d.

Mr. Glasspoole, the Miller and Yardsman, successfully applied for a post with the Whitechapel Union. His letter of resignation read:-

       Gentlemen,

          Permit me most respectfully to offer you my resignation of the office I now hold under you as Miller and Yardsman, at the same time be pleased to accept my grateful acknowledgement for all your kindness, particularly for your assistance which has enabled me to obtain the situation which I aspired to.

       I remain,

       Your obedient servant gentlemen,

          Henry Glasspoole.

This member of the artisan classes certainly knew how to pen a letter.

Workhouse children continued to be apprenticed out:-

4th. May, '47: *'The Clerk to write to the Guardians of Orsett Union to know if they would consent to the binding of William Taplin, aged 14 years, and Thomas Taplin, aged 13 years, the children by a former marriage of Mary White, belonging to Mucking parish, the elder boy to Mr. Read of Barking, fisherman, and Mr. Merchant, of the same place, fisherman'.*

(The younger boy presumably to the latter).

The children of the House had earlier caused a stir when the Matron discovered them passing love letters, or as she put it *'Very improper letters between the boys and girls of the House'*. Two letters were produced, one written by John Hammond to Fanny Turner, and one from Alexander Ashford to Maria Ballard. Summoned before the Board, the boys admitted their guilt, but like children found out everywhere, everyone started blaming everyone else. They said the girls sent the letters first. The girls said that another girl, called Emma Bray, who had *'left the House yesterday'*, had actually written the letters to the boys

All were given the statutory severe reprimand, and the Chaplain, the rev. Donkin, suggested moving the shoemaker's shop from the boys yard on account of the bad language used by Riley, the shoemaker, and his boy apprentice, Brown.

The Workhouse was not beyond growing a little wheat on its own account:-
5th. Oct. '47: *'Received £9 for wheat grown in the garden, being 3 Quarters at 60/-d; and £3 for 2 loads of straw'*.
The following Spring came the entry: *'Seeds for garden and cultivation of Workhouse land: £6.*
19th. Sept. '48. Among the Quarterly tenders accepted was Robert Pinfold's offer to sweep the chimneys for one year for £4; and Mr. Lake's undertaking to keep in repair the five clocks in the sum of £1.10.0d.

Early in March '49, a cheque for £1.10.0d was paid to Mr. Haws, the Workhouse porter (and gatekeeper) for *'Injury done to his clothes by Thomas Staines, who applied to the Board for relief'*. Does this enigmatic entry mean that, refused admittance to the House for Relief, the poor man became so frustrated with the Porter that he went for him?

Foundations were being dug for the new St. Edward's

As well as a constant stream of farms being bought and sold, other going concerns came on to the market as well:
From the Chelmsford Chronicle:-

THE BELL PUBLIC HOUSE.
Smithery and Premises.
Upminster, Essex.

Shuttleworth & Sons are instructed to SELL by AUCTION on Tuesday Auguast 13th., in two lots, a FREEHOLD ESTATE comprising THE BELL, a large and very substantial public house with extensive yard, garden and offices advantageously situate in the village of Upminster.
Also a substantial dwelling house, with large Smithery, with yards, sheds, gardens, and appurtenances adjoining The Bell, in the occupation of Messrs. Clarke and Eldred at rents amounting to £65 per annum.
May be viewed, and printed Particulars with Conditions had at The Bell aforesaid, and the White Hart, Romford.

The Public Health Act and Cholera.
Workhouse to Infirmary.
The Hungry Forties.

125

church, and the graves were disturbed. This was June '49, and with cholera rife, complaints were laid under the Public Health Act concerning *'The large heap of putrid matter, bones and earth deposited in the rear of the churchyard, and the continual pestiferous effluvia arising from the disturbed graves and the removal of coffins and bodies which are inefficiently re – interred'*.

Special complaint about all this was made by one Robert Wallis, who lived in an adjoining house. A Committee from the Board made an immediate inspection, including closely questioning the men working there. They could find nothing to uphold the complaint, even though it was a hot summer's day. In fact every precaution was being taken, including the liberal use of chloride of lime. There was however, in the yard at the back of Mr. Wallis' house,' *An open drain of a really offensive and unwholesome description which ought to be immediately attended to by the owner of the property'*. Hoist by his own Petard!

And so the entries continuously unfold; a diary of the events in the life of the Workhouse.

The mill began to show signs of wear. As ever, someone put in the lowest tender. It was Mr. White, who put in a new floor to the outer mill house, and a new stone floor to the mill house proper at 7/6d. A square yard.

19th. March, '50: Among tenders for supplies was one for Arrowroot: Mr. Scruby (grocer) 1/-d a lb. It was an old fashioned food for feeding to invalids.

26th. March, '50: Mr. Miller, Relieving Officer, took a week's holiday. In fourteen years, this was the first ever recorded for a Relieving Officer.

15th. October, '50: John Rust appointed new Miller and Yardsman.

17th. December, '50: Tenders for supplies included brandy at

Although I can find no bill anywhere, there was an agreement with a Mr. Siggers to supply a black horse to draw the (two wheeled) hearse belonging to the Workhouse.

His charges varied according to the distance to the various parish churches:-

Romford:	1/6d.
Upminster:	2/6d.
Dagenham:	3/6d.
Barking:	5/-d
Gt. Warley:	5/6d
Wennington:	6/-d.

Paupers were of course returned to their own parishes for burial.

20/- a gallon, and gin at 8/3d. a gallon. Nothing to do with Christmas. Christmas was never alluded to. It was for those in pain or terminally ill; a tot would be administered to alleviate their suffering or to help them to sleep.

25th. February, '51: Just four months after taking up his post, John Rust announced his marriage to Maria Hazeltine, the Workhouse cook, Did the Board congratulate them both and rejoice in their nuptials? After all, here was material for tomorrow's master and matron of a Workhouse. Did they? No! - they may have wanted to share a room together in the House and that would have threatened the discipline of the place, so it was deemed advisable that they should quit, and both parties were given a month's notice!

These then, were the concerns, great and small, of the Guardians and the staff and the inmates of Oldchurch Workhouse in 1850. What of the towns and parishes?

If you could have stood at this time on that bluff of high ground on the edge of the village green at Havering-atte-Bower and looked across that panoply of fields and villages of the Romford Union, stretching down to the Thames and to Barking; and seen not just the view, but into the hearts and minds of its men and women as they busied themselves about their lives; what then would they have had to show for themselves?

Out there, in the world at large, Parliament had doubled its electorate with the Great Reform Act. It had passed the Municipal Reform Act, setting up elected councils in the great northern industrial towns. There were Factory Acts , Penny Post, Repeal of the Corn Laws, Re-introduction of Income Tax, the lowering of the duties on foods, raw materials and dozens of everyday items, and in 1848 the Public Health Act was passed. We must not forget either, The Poor Law Amendment Act that gave birth to the Union itself.

It may well have been that the great majority of our folk

could neither write nor read; but some, a growing number could, and did, and talked one to another. So people were aware, many perhaps subconsciously, that they lived at a time of ever hastening social change. Thus the times, in spite of the poverty and despair, bred too a feeling of hope and optimism, enthusiasm and opportunity, that infected every man, be he a great fishing smack owner, or a man who had borrowed ten shillings to set up selling fish from door to door; be he the developer of Dagenham Lake, or a simple farm worker following his master's instructions on the four course crop rotation.

It made sense to belong to the Medical Club. Parents were beginning to realise the need to scrimp and save the pennies to send their children to learn to read and write. The men who attended the Literary and Mechanics Institute in the evening were eager to learn too. To me, all the evidence suggests that the people of the Romford Union had entered Victoria's era of 'self help' with just as much spirit as anyone in the land.

Among the tens of thousands of us who live today within the bounds of those erstwhile parishes of the Romford Union, not many, I will wager, can trace their lineage back directly some six or seven generations to ancestors living in the parishes then, at the dawn of the year of the Great Exhibition. Nevertheless it is my belief that many of us will recognise the optimism and resolve to forge ahead that had been kindled in the breasts of those men and women there on the northern banks of the Thames, in spite of the hardships of the times.

And when you reflect on it, it is the force that drives us still.

The Gatekeeper's Lodge as it is Today.

POSTSCRIPT.

Of course, the Workhouse didn't cease to function after 1851. It remained operational right through until the work of the Guardians was taken over by Essex County Council.

The last Board meeting was held on Tuesday 25th. March, 1930 - Quarter Day - businesslike as usual, with Mr. E.G. Bratchell, builder, in the Chair, and all forty eight members present.

On that day, when the bank balances were handed over to the County administration, the Minutes record that there were 758 inmates in the Institution, with a further 193 in Suttons Home for Old People, and no fewer than 148 children being cared for in the Scattered Homes.

On that day too, Oldchurch Hospital, as it had come to be known, was also taken over by the County. Greatly enlarged since the erection of those two ten bedded wards back in June 1848, and now boasting operating theatres and an X-ray department, it was caring for 545 patients.

Even as early as 1851 the function and running of the Workhouse had begun to change. Set up in the name of efficiency and economy, this austere, forbidding Workhouse building had been originally put up as part of a nationwide measure to cure a desperate problem - the soaring costs of the Poor Rate. However, by the middle of the century the more inhuman features of the regime were already being abolished.

Many things contributed to this progressive change:-
Britain held a clear lead in the world race for industrialisation and all that that meant in terms of jobs and earnings; The Great Exhibition of 1851 symbolised this for us.

The constrictive Corn Laws had been repealed, and helped not a little by the introduction of steel hulled ships, export and import business boomed.

The gold rushes in America and Australia led to an all round increase in the amount of money in circulation.

Parliamentary Acts of 1856 and '62 introduced Laws of Limited Liability, encouraging enterprise.

The Post Office Savings Bank was set up in 1861; and thrift was the watchword.

Whilst agricultural workers didn't benefit greatly, the majority of the population began to share in this prosperity, and average 'real' wages rose by a third between 1850 and 1875. Agriculture itself was experiencing a golden age; prices were stable, and there was a rapidly growing population to feed. Agricultural Shows promoted advances in animal breeding and crop culture, including the use of fertilisers such as Superphosphates, that by-product of the new methods of steel making which were keeping us ahead of the rest of the world.

Field draining was practiced widely, with local brickmakers, as we have seen, making the hollow clay drainage pipes to be laid herringbone fashion in the subsoil.

The railways, which in themselves had created many, many jobs, now made the movement of farm produce to the towns quicker and cheaper. And it was in the towns where the population was growing; not least in the two towns of the Romford Union.

By 1871, Barking had gone from 9036 to 12, 523, and Romford had almost doubled to 8293. Rainham and Dagenham too had grown markedly. Even though the numbers in the outlying villages had not changed greatly, the overall increase for the ten parishes in the Union was from 19, 521 in 1831, to 29,862 by 1871. This growth continued exponentially, especially in Barking, which by the turn of the century had a total of 104,015 souls if we include Ilford Ward, which was now a town in its own right - a product of the urbanisation brought about by the railway.

Whilst coal and steel may well have been at the heart of England, England's heart was becoming less and less steely. As the century progressed, parliamentary reform and increased social legislation proceed apace.

The original Poor Law Commissioners at Somerset House were replaced in 1847, first by the Poor Law Board, which became the Local Government Board in 1871, and this in turn eventually became the Ministry of Health.

In 1888 County Councils were created, and in 1894 the Rural and District Councils of Romford came into being. These elected councils took on more and more of the work that had originally been foisted on to the shoulders of the Board of Guardians.

The Reform Act, passed in 1867, gave the vote to town workmen, and in 1885 John Westlake, Liberal, was the first elected M.P. for the area; covering Havering, Romford, Dagenham, Ilford, Barking and East Ham.

On the social side, a long stream of Factory Acts were passed limiting the employment of children and women, and restricting the number of hours they worked; and all now enforced by Factory Inspectors.

There were progressive improvements in Public Health measures. Even soap was cheaper.

In a word, the plight of the working classes and the poor was steadily being approached in a more radical way. England was along way from today's Welfare State, but the public conscience was aroused; a start was being made.

So, when the Agricultural Depression took hold, which was to last right through from 1875 to the outbreak of war in 1914, we find that the luckless agricultural labourer, once the focus of the attentions of the New Poor Law Act, and now reduced to a small proportion of the total workforce compared with the one in six of the 1830's, was no longer pauperised or demoralised as of yore; other help was at hand.

It may be that the Workhouse was still a place of last resort, especially if you were old or infirm.
It may be that 'You'll end up in the Workhouse' could still be used as a threat to the shiftless; but the advancing century had robbed it of its imperative.
The dawning twentieth century would bring Old Age Pensions and National Insurance, and the hectic, callous days that have been the subject of this book would be consigned to history.
England, in her compassion, and with her sense of fairness….